The
Psychotropic
MIND

The
Psychotropic
MIND

The World according to
Ayahuasca, Iboga, and Shamanism

Jeremy Narby
Jan Kounen
Vincent Ravalec

Translated by Jon E. Graham

Park Street Press
Rochester, Vermont • Toronto, Canada

Park Street Press
One Park Street
Rochester, Vermont 05767
www.ParkStPress.com

Park Street Press is a division of Inner Traditions International

Originally published in French under the title *Plantes et chamanisme, Conversations autour de l'ayahuasca & de l'iboga* by Mama Editions
First U.S. edition published in 2010 by Park Street Press

Note to the Reader: The information provided in this book is for educational, historical, and cultural interest only and should not be construed as a guide to or advocacy of the use or ingestion of ayahuasca or iboga, or any other hallucinogenic plant substance. Neither the author nor the publisher assume any responsibility for physical, psychological, or social consequences resulting from the ingestion of these substances or their derivatives.

Library of Congress Cataloging-in-Publication Data
Narby, Jeremy.
  [Plantes et chamanisme. English]
  The psychotropic mind : the world according to ayahuasca, iboga, and shamanism / Jeremy Narby, Jan Kounen, Vincent Ravalec ; translated by Jon E. Graham. — 1st U.S. ed.
      p. cm.
  "Originally published in French under the title: Plantes et chamanisme."
  Includes index.
  Summary: "Conversations on shamanism and mind-altering plants by filmmaker Jan Kounen, anthropologist Jeremy Narby, and writer/filmmaker Vincent Ravalec"—Provided by publisher.
  ISBN 978-1-59477-312-9
  1. Psychotropic plants. 2. Shamanism. 3. Ibogaine—Psychotropic effects.
  4. Ayahuasca—Psychotropic effects. I. Kounen, Jan, 1964– II. Ravalec, Vincent, 1962– III. Title.
  BF207.N3713 2010
  154.4—dc22
                                                                    2009034337

Printed and bound in the United States by Lake Book Manufacturing

10 9 8 7 6 5 4 3 2 1

Text design and layout by Virginia Scott Bowman
This book was typeset in Garamond Premier Pro and Gill Sans with Bodoni Antiqua and Gill Sans as display typefaces

Contents

Introduction

The seed was sowed in 2006 when Tigrane Hadengue conceived the idea for a book born from the meeting of three seemingly very different individuals who shared one thing in common: the practice of ayahuasca shamanism.

Jeremy Narby is an anthropologist. Beneath a head of unruly hair is a mind that combines the juvenile and the rigorous. Now more than ten years ago, he wrote a book that has attained cult status and has been published in a dozen languages since that time, one that greatly contributed to bringing ayahuasca into public awareness. He is forty-eight years old.

Vincent Ravalec, author of several dozen highly popular books, has been alternately described as a rock writer and Tintin journalist who writes about wisdom plants. Thin and discreet, sporting a broken nose, he is forty-six years old.

Jan Kounen is a filmmaker and an author. His films (several of which have been inspired by ayahuasca shamanism) have enjoyed much notoriety and triggered controversy. Impulsive, warmhearted, and with a clean-shaven head, he is forty-three years old.

Their rendezvous was set for March 12, 2007. Vincent Ravalec suggested a list of themes to discuss (which was expanded by Jeremy Narby):

1. What is the genesis of your interest in shamanism?
2. Risks and dangers connected to shamanism and the consumption of psychotropic substances.
3. Gain—or not—after several years of hindsight.

1

4. Is it possible for a Westerner to take a truly shamanic approach today?
5. The relationship between civilization and nature.
6. The sciences and archaic practices.
7. The pertinence of divulging this information to "the public at large."
8. Possible meaning for the future of our contemporaries and our planet.
9. The dark side of shamanism: sorcery.
10. The hygiene (mental and physical) of power.
11. What about healing? Is shamanism effective?
12. Shamanism, man and woman.

Their meeting took place in an apartment in the eleventh arrondissement of Paris. The three fellows took their seats at a round table. Their audience consisted of Tigrane Hadengue, iconoclastic publisher, and Michka, a woman with a taste for wilderness as well as an author and a publisher.

The three companions spoke from two that afternoon until well into the night (with several breaks, including one for dinner).

The conversation duly recorded, each of them returned home.

The recording was then transcribed. During the following months, Michka whipped the text into shape and then sent it on to these three individuals, who made a few minor revisions here and there.

This became Conversation I, the first chapter of this book titled Ayahuasca and Iboga, because, taking advantage of the hindsight provided by reading this first text, they decided to see each other again.

The second meeting took place on October 22, 2007. It was also recorded, transcribed, put into shape, and then slightly revised by the authors, becoming the second chapter: The Mysteries Encountered.

The ambience of these encounters was quite distinct. The conversations show evidence of a subtle quality: the three authors brought with them a way of listening, a simplicity, an honesty, and a humor that ended up being as eloquent as the words they spoke.

It is now for the reader to judge.

ONE

Ayahuasca and Iboga

THE DANGERS AND THE BENEFITS

VINCENT: The question I ask myself is, Why do a book on this subject? Will it be of any use to anyone? Before we go further, I would like us to ask ourselves this question, because I have already done a book on iboga, as well as contributed various texts on psychotropic substances, and for the time being, the consequences, the return that I've seen, have not been very positive.

I am extremely dubious, all the more so as ayahuasca and iboga are both now illegal in France. But beyond the legal or penal aspect of things, from an existential human perspective, is reading a book on this subject going to give anything to anyone?

Excuse me for getting a little preachy, but I think we have to raise the basic question of why we do things, what it is we want to do, for ourselves and for others, in this dimension as in others.

I think that the people who have access to this kind of knowledge, like the people who have access to science, should have a greater ethical consideration than others because they have more responsibility. Personally, I ask myself a lot of questions. Having a very small amount of public exposure with my books, and especially since my book on iboga, I have been giving a lot of thought to how I speak about my experiences.

I think that you, Jeremy, were faced with this with *The Cosmic Serpent*.

JEREMY: Yes, this is something that has been in my mind for years.

VINCENT: And what is your position?

JEREMY: It is true that with *Intelligence in Nature,* I made a sort of "sharp tack left." I pulled away from anything that might encourage people while trying to remain faithful to the subject—the subject being, as far as I am concerned, the situation of the indigenous peoples of the Amazon.

The fact is that these people and their knowledge have been scorned for centuries, and psychoactive plants are at the center of their way of knowing the world and that, well, that contradicts the Western paradigm. This is already interesting in itself; it is even too interesting to avoid talking about it. We are dealing with a case of epistemological blockage.

The fact of talking about it appeared constructively subversive in this world to me; and at the same time, I had no desire to send young Western sheep to hurl themselves into the wolf's jaws and create more confusion. For example, I carefully avoid taking ayahuasca in Europe, that's clear.

In my past books, I gave the floor to shamans who explained that the use of ayahuasca is ambiguous and that it also includes questions of power.

I have the impression that it is a good thing to talk about as long as it is done in a detailed, balanced manner, with both light and darkness, and most importantly, putting it back into a context of learning.

In the Amazon, they do not talk about these as hallucinogens but as tools for communicating with the other species. Ayahuasca is first and foremost a means of transcending the barrier that separates us from other species and keeps us from communicating with plants and animals in our visions. I continue to think that in the West what we are dealing with is an understanding deficit, and I like the idea of putting our three heads together and looking for a new way to talk about these things, in a way that honors them.

These plants are tools, power tools, that can be productive and also dangerous at the same time. Therefore, the more intelligence we can transmit about how to use them, the better. I think it is first and foremost a question of discouraging people, of saying: "Listen, this is not everybody's cup of tea. Watch out, these are deep waters, you need to be completely informed before diving in, this is like sailing on the high seas."

But I love sailing on the high seas! There are taboos in our culture concerning psychoactive plants. In fact, they are illegal in most Western countries. And, yes, I do rather want to break the silence. I find that we are, the three of us, people of words and communication; and if we three are not capable of finding the words to begin a conversation about the use and abuse of these plants, I don't know who is going to do it. . . .

VINCENT: And you, Jan, what do you think?

JAN: I think more or less the same thing. Once you have been in contact (and I am speaking about my own personal case) with . . . what I was going to call a science, a traditional medicine that, while restoring your balance, causes you to perceive the relationship with nature in another way, well, we see how enormously we have been conditioned.

When I began my investigation and went to visit the shamans I thought, in terms of belief systems, that they were a little crazy in the sense that they believed in far-out things. But they still managed to heal, a priori, and to perceive things differently with the aid of plants.

Once our encounter took place and was so strong, I was actually exposed in a strong and repeated manner to a radical system shift. You see the world differently, and in a fairly clear way. It is, in fact, a way of healing yourself.

VINCENT: Yes, yes . . .

JAN: It reconciles you with such important things as suffering, death, and everything that surrounds you in nature. Starting from there, my work has been directed not toward saying that everyone should take ayahuasca, but rather as the dominant culture, it was our duty to see where it led. To at least make the information available that the Indians are not only a remnant of the past or a lost paradise, or good savages.

While we were advancing by weaving matter and building up our civilization and our way of thinking about the world, they were advancing, as human beings, in another direction. And the sum of knowledge they have of certain domains seems superior to ours. So there should be at least the recognition of a knowledge that we do not have. I made some films in this direction, *D'autre mondes* and *Blueberry,** and I think this is the reason I am here at this table with you.

I want to at least attempt to get some information into circulation. To say: "Just look. Then you may believe or not believe, but here is some information that won't allow you to make the transition from one system to another, nor to suddenly look at the world with different eyes, but at least will allow you to see that there are systems of understanding in the world that are different and complementary." It is my deep impression today that indigenous people are ahead of us in certain areas of pure cognition, interspecies relations, and on ways of comprehending the phenomena connected to death and to tangible phenomena.

It is quite hard to communicate these things because we do not have any key. So it is going to have to be through testimony, the translation of states of consciousness into words, which is to say the transition from a nonverbal language to a verbal one that is quite reductive and difficult to grasp.

This is where, artistically speaking, the game becomes interesting for me. I am not a word person; I am rather a person who uses the language of images. It is quite difficult to talk about visions because it's a nonverbal language; words are not the tool to do this. This is the boundary I see limiting this discussion.

But in any case it is worth trying. And with words, we can weave in other subjects that connect with traditional medicine: the dangers, the whys, the politics, the social aspects. . . .

It is extremely hard to communicate this kind of knowledge in a tangible manner to someone who does not have this experience. It is as if these plants awaken a new sense. Talking about this sense is like imagining that sound does not exist for someone and trying to describe

---

*[Released in English as *Other Worlds* and *Renegades. —Trans.*]

what it is like to hear. . . . It is quite hard if the person has never heard a thing! And if the person doesn't even have a desire to listen to discussions about sound, describing to him or her how a philharmonic orchestra plays a symphony . . .

So there it is: hearing is possible and there is something in each of us that is closed, which individual consciousness can open.

[Silence.]

VINCENT: I agree with both of you on this point. For me this is obvious. What I'm wondering about is the pertinence of this kind of discussion. In fact, I think it can bring us to further considerations inasmuch as it's been quite a while since the three of us were confronted with a different culture, in the strong experiences that you have alluded to, strong in comparison with our habitual system of perception. Then to see what kind of conclusions we can draw today, and if they are sufficiently positive and interesting, both for us and for those that surround us. We all know people who have taken part in experiences like these and what effect—positive or negative—it had on their lives. Let's see if it is useful to communicate this information and what warnings we can raise, and how best to present it.

The perceptual system of human beings today is quite restricted, in the sense that it stops at itself, at the image it has of man. The universe and the cosmos practically do not exist; nature is becoming more and more abstract. So, for me, it was a kind of opening to something much more vast.

But it is true that with the feedback I got after the publication of my book on iboga . . . I am fairly perplexed, in fact, because I am not at all sure what should be done. . . . There you have it.

These experiences are not well perceived, and I raise the question without having the answer: is talking about them a good or a bad thing? Knowing that, in perhaps a silly way, I think it is better to try to do a good thing rather than a bad thing.

So then what is a good thing and what is a bad thing? We can debate this subject for a long time, but in the specific case of an initiatory path founded on plants, a good thing simply moves in the direction of one's personal evolution, in a very basic way. The people who go through such an experience, even if it is painful, call into question their conceptual patterns, their way of looking at the world, their life habits—in the end, will this experience bring them something better than they had before?

When I look at people I know who have tried ayahuasca or iboga, I sometimes ask myself: "Did this do anything for them or did it make them, not necessarily stupid but . . . not necessarily better?"

For ayahuasca, Jeremy, you wrote a book that, I think, has led many people to try it. In my own case, I wrote a book with two other people on iboga, *Bois sacré,* that had much less of an impact but all the same influenced people to try it.

I got phone calls, people wrote me . . . people who were worse off afterward. Was this something temporary or was something not working?

So I think if we are really going to do this book, there are some important things to get straight: one, provide some potential conceptual keys.

With the iboga book I felt as if I had truly been entrusted with the mission of a bridge builder: to see how it would be possible to build a bridge between our Western conceptual system and a conceptual system that has nothing in common with it. And to discover what keys could be borrowed from it.

I think it is important to point this out because each of us in our own way have found the keys appropriate for us; if not we would not be here today to discuss them. And even if they are not the same keys, they can provide ideas through the phenomenon of analogy.

Number two, the warning. In other words, people arrive with different conceptual systems, conceptual systems that have been constructed with history.

When we see people in Africa or the Amazon who take psychotropic substances and actually have access to other modes of communication and power systems, as you have said, Jeremy, these are people facing a life that is not at all like our own. They are predators, hunters. They have that inside them, they have another way of relating to each other, another lifestyle—an extremely hard lifestyle.

A Westerner can truly be eaten alive. We have to pay attention to this because, without going into details, people should know that this can be dangerous!

I've seen people going over there totally naive, thinking that "everyone is beautiful, everyone is kind." It so happens when you are living in a jungle, this is completely untrue. There is danger everywhere. The people there are warriors first of all, they are hunters. And if we are turning to these peoples, it is because they still have these qualities. Even though we may still have them, too. It is important that people understand this.

That's what I have to say. I don't know what you think about this.

JEREMY: But absolutely!

JAN: A real clarification has to be made: What is a shaman? I have noticed that there is a lot of confusion between an Indian or Tibetan sage and a shaman. The shaman is not a sage: there is a kind of knowledge there, a wisdom even, but he or she is not a sage in the sense that we've known before. When people draw parallels with the culture of the 1970s, they begin to discover, little by little, that shamans are quite different from what they thought. And it is these preconceived notions that are going to cause problems.

VINCENT: I think you are touching on something there that is quite important. There is one definition for shaman that I like a lot: the shaman is the someone capable of restoring order and harmony in the group. Someone who, when there is a dysfunction in a group—a tribe—he or she is capable of resynchronizing the elements of the group with nature and the cosmos.

This is a definition that suits me really well. And I also think this is the challenge facing modern man today. We have the capability to jump back into the past, to visit cultures that do not operate like ours and have very different systems of interaction. If we do this book, we should be able to show evidence of harmonization. We should be capable of establishing harmony between cultures smoothly, and specifically with a plan for reparations, which is quite important—because after all, the world has been constructed from a bloodbath. The Indians have been massacred, Africa was invaded; all of these things form part of our history, they are part of our collective unconscious.

When I took part in these experiences, it was with a specific desire to restore harmony, knowing that the conflicts of history are made to be reabsorbed, at some point, and that culture and knowledge are good tools for doing this.

JEREMY: So . . . it's true that we should have all kinds of things to talk about. But then it seems to me that we are already fully into the subject although we have not yet finished discussing the rules of the game.

I would be ready to roll up my sleeves and talk about the definition of shaman, the concept, how it has come into the European cultures; and we could talk about it all night, but it seems to me that we first need to get past the phase: Why create this book?

Are we going to do this book? If yes, why? And then, how? If we say: "We are not going to do this book," then simply shut the tape recorder off and that's that.

But it seems to me that the three of us are all in agreement to have a long conversation today that will be recorded and can become the basis for a manuscript; and if it becomes obvious that one of the three of us is against publication of the text that results, well, then we will just drop it.

JAN: I hear what Vincent is saying, and I think that this book can be a unique opportunity to attack the problems that have come up between the West and the jungle of shamanism. Actually there are some things that are typically left out. For example, I have not spoken about the witchcraft side of shamanism, its negative side. I got together with you because I think we all have things to say about what lies beneath the direct experience of things that don't belong to the world of philosophy or visions, but concrete things. You talk about keys, but I want to talk about the method and the way we relate to this kind of experience in a very simple manner. I could talk about the times that I messed up, for example, and felt terrible. The better I understand these things, the better my ongoing active relationship with Shipibo shamanism has become—the only form of shamanism I'm familiar with.

There are negative experiences surrounding shamanism, things I do not normally talk about that could be shared, and why not? If we have a true duty toward the phenomenon itself and to our own culture, it is to say: "Look, there is both good and bad here." It's our responsibility to our readers as well. But it requires that we really open up. You, for example, Vincent, I find it great that you are so open about your qualms: "I came up against a wall, why?" That might help others to avoid hitting the same wall. It's happened to me, too; I admit it. It is not all black or white. In this sense, I agree it is good to push a little deeper into those areas where we feel cornered, knowing we can always read everything over and that the object of the game is to keep even the things that make us uneasy. This would make a more interesting and original book.

VINCENT: So can we get back to the small list of questions I suggested? After a break.

[Break]

SHAMANISM

JEREMY: Vincent, what was the genesis of your interest in shamanism?

VINCENT: The genesis of my interest in shamanism is quite simple: I was a teenager in the 1970s. And even if they appear hazy and slightly messy today, to say the least, the 1970s brought an enormous quantity of myths: science fiction, comic books, access to global spirituality, which had been around since the beginning of the twentieth century, with the theosophists and all that, but it really grew then also because of the globalization of travel.

When I was an adolescent I saw people returning from South America or from ashrams in India. That really fed my imaginations. And when I got a little older I told myself that the time was now or never to go see if what I had read was true, if there were really people who could levitate like in Tintin in Tibet, if there were really sorcerers in the forest, things like that. On the one hand I was motivated by basic curiosity, and on the other a deeper more existential curiosity. I thought that behind all this there might be doors you could push open and that behind these doors there might be a different kind of knowledge. I set off on my travels with total candor and naïveté.

JEREMY: You grew up in the city?

VINCENT: I've always been an urbanite. I grew up in the Parisian suburbs. I was born in Paris—I think this intersects with other questions we can bring up later—and for me life in the city was a kind of enigma. So, even if I did not think of it like this at the time, it was a way of going to see what our origins were.

I think that this is one of the most interesting things about shamanism, this sort of leap in the collective consciousness of our planet. In a few hours and for relatively little expense, one can pop back into the past, a world that when all is said and done is not that far from us.

Without even entering into a shamanic experience right away, just seeing what the people of Africa, of the Amazon, are facing—which must be close to our own situation several centuries or several thousand years ago—that alone already causes quite a substantial shock. It is also a chance to change our relationship to time because it is easier to see where we come from.

So that's the genesis of my interest in shamanisn: it is an adolescent mythology fed by a relatively cheap imaginary realm, gleaned from comic books and the J'ai Lu (*L'aventure Mystérieuse*), Robert Laffont (*Les Mondes parallèles*) collections.

And what is really funny is that I actually went to the places I read about in these books. For example, the Nazca thing—I think it was Pierre Charron who wrote the book about the small stones with the winged dinosaurs and the extraterrestrial landing strip. Well, with Marc Caro—who is a filmmaker—there I was! [Laughs.] We went to the guy's museum to see if this thing was real. We read that when we were fourteen or fifteen years old; it was like following a dream.

[Silence.]

JEREMY: When I was a child, growing up in the Montreal suburbs, I saw Indians in the reservations around the city, and they actually scared me. The attitude of the people around me was to say: "Those people are like gypsies, those people are thieves, they cannot be trusted. You need to keep your distance when going through the Indian reservations." In fact, we whites in our cars were ashamed, and we looked away. I was scared of the Indians, and it was not my fault, my culture was racist.

We left for Switzerland when I was ten years old, and it wasn't Indians that interested me then but dolphins, which seemed so intelligent and endowed with awareness. I consulted Robert Stenuit, a Belgian writer who has written about dolphins, about how to become a dolphinologist. When I was twelve or thirteen I wrote him a letter and he answered saying that I would have to go to college and study science, with an emphasis on chemistry and mathematics, if I wanted to study dolphins. It was a little discouraging.

When I turned eighteen, the thing that most interested me was the problem of the rich and poor—I was still a long way from altered states of consciousness.

I ended up studying history in college. At nineteen, I developed an interest for the history of madness, following my reading of Thomas Szasz's book *The Myth of Mental Illness* and Michel Foucault's *Histoire de la folie à l'âge classique*.

One of my father's friends advised me, when he heard that I wanted to do my bachelor's thesis on the history of madness, to go visit the psychiatrist Humphry Osmond. He was the man who coined the word *psychedelic* and who administered the mescaline to Aldous Huxley that would encourage him to write *The Doors of Perception*.

So, when I was nineteen I spent a month in Alabama at the home of Humphry Osmond. I went with him to the hospital every day and then spent the evenings with him in his library. He showed me all his books and talked at length to me about LSD. Because in the beginning, in the 1950s, LSD was a tool science considered potentially useful, with all kinds of capabilities, like the ability to cure alcoholism.

It was in Humphry Osmond's library that I began to read everything concerning LSD, mescaline, and hallucinogens. It is true that this was a fascinating subject for someone interested in states of consciousness, how the brain works, what its molecules are, and the worlds to which it gives access.

After this, when I was twenty and had gone back to my university in England, I began not only devouring all the books I could find on the subject but also the mushrooms that grew in the fields. This basically means that you can read, but you can also try. It was possible to take mushrooms one day, read Castaneda the next, and say to yourself: "Yes, there is a knowledge like the one the shamans talk about. There is something that appears quite bizarre in comparison to Western consumer society."

You go to the supermarket on mushrooms and you begin to deconstruct the reality that is right before your eyes. You say: "What are these things all wrapped in plastic; where do they come from? What are these chickens cut into pieces? Just what is this bizzaro industrial world that is my normal reality and that I am presently watching like a strange movie?"

Every time I took hallucinogens (psilocybin mushrooms and LSD) it was a huge, almost philosophical slap that made me consider all the big questions. What is life? What is culture? What are the values society injects us with even when we are not aware it is doing so? And besides, how do I know this? So many questions!

It was clear that there was something that remained poorly understood by our culture. Something that was pertinent for someone who took an interest in the inequalities of the world—I was a Marxist at this time—for someone interested in the inequalities of class, race, and gender. . . . So I then quit history to begin studying anthropology.

It was a question of radically rethinking the world, focusing on the inequities between human beings, and trying to see how this situation was constructed historically, culturally. A question of analyzing everything while at the same time using these tools for altering consciousness in order to get out of my culture and to try to see it from above. The goal was to change the world, in fact.

JAN: And the shamans?

JEREMY: No, as an anthropologist.

JAN: Yes, but the shamans?

JEREMY: Oh, yeah! The shamans . . . thank you.

As a young anthropologist, I had begun taking an interest in the "development of the third world." I wanted to achieve a critique of the policies of the large international development banks, like the World Bank. At this time, in the early 1980s, these banks were investing hundreds of millions of dollars to build roads penetrating the Amazon in order to expropriate the native peoples and replace them with colonists to raise livestock. All this in the name of "development." I decided to go to the Amazon to see the conflict between the bulldozers and millions of World Bank dollars versus barefoot people with arrows. It was two completely different concepts. From the Indians' point of view, development was not razing the jungle, bringing in livestock, and evicting folk; it was recognition of the fact that these people had knowledge about their forest, that they knew how to use it without destroying it. This is what development is: recognize the territorial rights of the indigenous people and work together with them to ensure that this fragile and valuable environment continues to exist.

It was a question at this time of taking action as a politically engaged anthropologist, going to live with the Indians of the Peruvian Amazon, there where the bulldozers were coming, and demonstrate that they had pertinent knowledge about the jungle.

So the little boy who was scared of Indians in Montreal found himself, in October 1984, in an Ashaninca village, and it is true that I was scared I might get scalped the first evening there. This kind of prejudice is obviously completely stupid.

And then, little by little—this is what an anthropologist's work is all about—you start hanging out with the people, you spend days and weeks accompanying them. I was there to study what they knew about nature. In fact they knew all kinds of things, they knew all kinds of plants, and, in the end, all kinds of things proved to be true.

They say: "This plant accelerates the scarring of wounds." You have an injury, you take the plant, and yes, it accelerates the scarring of your wound. By virtue of leading my investigation and verifying their knowledge, I stumbled upon shamanism. This was because when you ask these people, "How do you know that," they say, "We have plants, ayahuasca, tobacco, toé, that our shamans take, and then they have visions. They see the essences, or spirits, that are common to all life-forms, and who give them information. Everything we know, we learned from nature spirits."

So here we have a different epistemology, with right at the center not microscopes, but plants that alter consciousness. This contradicts the principles of rationalism. Thus, as a rationalist, you find yourself in front of a mirror. You are placed in front of your own presuppositions. If this was all there was to it, it would still be interesting.

And after knocking on the door of shamanism and testing it, one tells oneself that there really is something to these altered states of consciousness. There is a source of knowledge.

And you, Jan. [Laughs.]

JAN: For me, it is a little like for Vincent in the sense that it was through novelists and the world of comic books that I encountered this. If I think back on it a little, the source of my meeting with shamanism was Frank Herbert's novel *Dune*. In this novel, there is a planet that has a spice; this spice alters consciousness and allows one to get information about the world, a force, a power.

I first read this novel when I was fourteen and kept rereading it— until I was eighteen, I think. At fourteen I didn't really understand it, but it spoke to me, a little like when seeing *2001: A Space Odyssey*—I saw it when I was eight years old—I did not get it, but it spoke to me.

I thought back to *Dune* and the spice when I met the shamans, telling myself that it was this book that brought me there. It's the feeling of carrying some information inside oneself—that one can weave a relationship with forms of intelligence, something that novels, science-fiction books, and comics do all the time. The fantastic speaks to us—speaks to me—not because it is a complete fantasy but because it has a profound truth, artistically woven together like a myth.

Therefore I would say that it was science-fiction novels—Jack Vance, Jodo/Moebius, Philip K. Dick—that began to weave this interest together. All of this was lying under the surface. I loved to read those books, and I loved the ideas. I loved the ideas.

After that there were films that put me on the path. Like Ken Russel's *Altered States.* Suddenly I started dreaming of going into a sensory deprivation tank; that spoke to me.

When I was fourteen I had my first encounter with the Indian world through the film *Little Big Man,* which depicted Indians in a totally new way. I did not quite get it in the beginning, but I did perceive that I was being told a different story, and I think it was this film that aroused my curiosity about the Indian world.

I find the educational power of cinema dizzying. I am not going to go into the depiction of Indians in films, but at this time American cinema was . . . you destroy a people, then to justify the genocide you fabricate stories that show them to be ignoble.

Fortunately from the heart of this culture emerged a being, in this case a director, an author, actors, a political will, in the very heart of the most dominant culture on the planet, to make an artistic work that is going to show another point of view. So history gets questioned a little.

All these phenomena occurred at the same time. We discovered science fiction, fantasy, Métal Hurlant* comic books, where fantasy and altered states of consciousness are adapted to fiction.

And I would say that my first experience not with shamanism but with altered consciousness (except for the anesthesia in the hospital during an operation) was much later. I smoked a joint when I was sixteen years old, a little grass. I did it at night with some buddies while watching the stars in the countryside thinking to myself: "Perhaps I am going to feel the stars?" Although I wasn't reading about it and didn't

---

*[*Métal hurlant* was a graphic novel journal. —*Trans.*]

have any specific education about psychotropic substances, I was simply moved by an instinctive desire. I didn't experience any great communion with the cosmos, but the intention was stated.

Jeremy, you talked about more political things being at the source. I would say that between the ages of fourteen and twenty, I had a strong metaphysical questioning. And when I entered art school it was with the desire to make films.

I let this desire penetrate me. I wanted to make films. I put all of my energy into this and into developing my imagination, and a kind of instinctive thought process. I sought to develop the tools needed to bring back images from the imaginary world and manufacture them.

Once I had made my first film, called *Dobermann*, I told myself: "Okay, I've made a movie. Now what I need, if I make another film, is to go deeply into a subject that interests me not just for the sake of shaking people up." I realized that for ten years I had abandoned reading *Dune* and lots of other things, my metaphysical interests, and I dove back into them.

That's when I encountered the writings of Huxley and Castaneda. At this time—less than ten years ago, when I was around thirty-four—I felt I had settled my score with religion through the appalling figure of the abbot in *Dobermann*. It was as if I had spit out my anger inspired by the religious phenomenon that had confronted me in my upbringing and the perception I had retained of it. I could read the Gospels again, I could read the Tibetans, I could read religious things.

I didn't get directly into shamanism and altered states of consciousness, but rather into meditation with the Tibetans and their texts and somewhat by the book by Matthieu Ricard and his first question: What is the nature of thought?

No one had ever asked me that. No one had ever said at school: "Look, thought is a tool, not for communication but so you can build, in a specific manner, your relationship to the world. Afterward, you will be able to communicate." Meditation, in other words the natural approach to the phenomenon known as thought—how to perceive it, how it germinates, where it comes from, how to have a perception of thought—no one ever talked about this in school. Then I asked myself: "Why isn't this the first thing they teach us?"

So this was how it started. As I began researching I suddenly had the desire to make a film on the subject. Not on meditation but on perceiving the world differently, transcendence—touching on altered states of consciousness.

Since I am a filmmaker, I told myself that a good way to study the matter would be to make a film about it.

In this search, I met shamans who represented a more baroque vision of cinema for me, in other words, the endangering of a character because he takes a substance, he is going to ingest a plant that puts him violently into an altered state of consciousness.

With movies it is possible to play with danger and intense perceptions of reality, which are the very nature of the cinema's tools. When you frame a close-up, you are perceiving a reality differently, you induce it. If, all at once, the soundtrack stops, you strip one meaning from it—the opposite if you change the sound. All cinema does is play with altered states of consciousness in the viewer. I had these tools; why not experiment with them?

There were two ways to do this. I looked at what happened in the '70s. I investigated further and found lots of people who were seekers and who had taken off without hesitation not from point zero, but without any specialist or guide in their own culture.

There were books, like yours in particular, Jeremy, that allowed me to see that there are in fact cultures, and thus individuals, who are familiar with these states and have been for thousands of years. To talk about these states, if they are not part of your culture, you are just going to make up fantasies about them.

If you want to make a film about amorous desire, and you've never made love, but you are a poet, a filmmaker, you could make a very beautiful film about desire, love, sharing. It will be interesting but it will be fantasy. Or else you can tell yourself: "Fine, I am going to have lots of experiences with lots of women, and I will glean lots of information from this and make a movie."

This is the trail I opted to follow for altered systems of consciousness. I went to see those who would be capable—this is my comfort zone—of guiding me rather than staying home all alone and taking ketamine or LSD. So I went to take ayahuasca.

In this case, there were several people and several books, including *The Cosmic Serpent,* that inspired my desire to go to the Amazon and take ayahuasca—I had already been with the Huichol for peyote.

There were people from my own culture who had adventured into the Amazon and assimilated bits of information, that had found their way to me. So this seemed like a safe system to me. In the same way that if I had to have surgery I perhaps wouldn't go to the Amazon. For surgery I would more likely go to a hospital here because we have more dealings with this kind of healing. But I was not going there to be healed; I went in search of metaphysical nebulosity to make a film. That is how I went to visit the Shipibo shamans.

Now to bring this to a close . . . When you decide to make a movie on a subject such as this and take off on an adventure to meet shamans, things do not turn out like you thought, and you do not find what you expected to find. That's the story.

JEREMY: Meaning?

JAN: Meaning that you leave with the idea of making a film, investigating states of consciousness, and gaining info. Once you are there and you've entered that world—and that's how it was for me, I don't know why, but I entered it quite quickly—this world alters you. It's not about making a movie anymore. At some point, you find yourself in front of your glass of ayahuasca. Already, before you even drink it, you are no longer a filmmaker gathering information; you are a human being facing an experience. And if you experience something, and it is strong, the next day the person you see in the mirror is not a filmmaker who had beautiful visions for making a film but a poor wretch who's been completely shaken up. . . .

JEREMY: . . . and who questions the fact of making a film . . .

JAN: . . . and who is telling himself that everything he has been told for thirty-five years about the nature of the reality of the human experience was way off the mark. That at thirty-five, he must completely reconsider his entire reality. And there . . . that's where it begins to turn bad. It is not necessarily a very good moment. Yet, the experience was magnificent! [Laughs.]

JEREMY: And the film's producer rings this guy on the phone. . . .

JAN: The film producer was extremely alarmed because I actually came back and told my producers: "Listen . . ." They were quite worried because they had spent a fair sum of money so that I could go to the Amazon.

I succeeded in convincing them to let me go. I had already visited the Huichol and made it back. When I returned, I dressed up as a Huichol when my producer came to see me at home and I greeted him: "My brother!" I saw his face freeze like: "Shit, Jan has lost it. Bye-bye!" And then I said: "Wait, I'm kidding!" [Laughs.]

Except when I returned from staying with the Shipibo, I wasn't wearing any necklaces or a costume, nothing. On the other hand, I said to them word for word: "Ariel, Thomas, everything is going great! Let me give you a hug! Forget the idea of making a movie; you have to come with me to the Amazon. We will make a movie in a couple years maybe. There are things that are much more important than making films!" This kept my producers from getting any sleep for a couple of weeks. But we eventually made a film because I changed my mind several weeks later. So . . . there's the answer to your question. [Laughs.]

JEREMY: All that makes a good story!

What made you change your mind later? Because, when you have experienced ayahuasca and experienced fundamental revelations, you say: "Stop, I want to change everything." But eventually you end up going back. What was it that made you go back to "reality"?

JAN: I have never come back to reality. [Laughs.]

I need to be a little more precise. What happened, as I said before, is all at once you're facing another reality that is too complex to put into words.

What is a human being? You have information on important things like death, the possibilities of encounters with other dimensions of reality that seem connected with this reality, but that I only learned about with the help of plants. This causes your profound ideas about reality, life, and all that to turn upside down. So it really fucks things up, even if the experiences are incredibly beautiful. I have to admit, I was completely lost when I came back. Maybe not lost but on the brink.

I did not realize how I was scaring everyone around me, because I was going to all my friends and saying: "Listen, guys, cinema is nothing, it is only an epiphenomenon. I have encountered something that is truly interesting; you have to come with me to the Amazon." It's true, that's how I was.

JEREMY: That's proselytism. . . .

JAN: I wouldn't say proselytism. It was something that was obvious. I was like Richard Dreyfuss in *Close Encounters of the Third Kind*. I did not meet extraterrestrials in the same way, but I was like him. I didn't build a glass mountain, but I was in a state of jubilation, of ecstasy. . . . I wanted others to profit from it. I just wasn't hearing the signals coming back.

People knew me as someone who always made movies, who was obsessed with cinema, who lived, ate, and shat cinema. And one of the things ayahuasca did with me was to make me aware that there was something else, in the life of a human being, than his imagination or his work as a filmmaker. There were other things like meeting people, traveling. . . .

So the first thing I said was that I wanted to stop making movies for a year, travel, and help everyone to experience different cultures. These are completely reasonable and natural ideas; with hindsight you would say they were even healthy. But our culture gets really scared by someone who has changed radically because he took some kind of drug with a sorcerer in the depths of the jungle. This is something I did not realize then, and it caused me problems for a while.

JEREMY: It seems to me that a messianic tendency is one of the risks, the dangers of this kind of experience. What do you think?

VINCENT: Personally, that is not part of my makeup.

JEREMY: But it is something you have observed in others, perhaps?

VINCENT: I think that starting from the time someone has had a strong experience, there is a tendency to want to share it. We can revisit this later in another category of questions that touches on this one: What is it that truly impels us to seek out this kind of experience and in what state of mind did one experience it, and continues to experience it, and possibly tries to transmit it?

Let me explain: I think there is something at the bottom of every individual like a small vibration. This vibration forms who we are becoming, and it pushes us to embrace this or that kind of experience. Because it is geographically remote, culturally disorientating, and hallucinatory, an experience like shamanism makes it so that in one stroke you are going to start vibrating differently, and the intention you hold in your deepest depths is going to determine how it develops. . . . So this is also what is going to show through in your "messianic" ambition if you have one. This means you have to be incredibly clear with yourself; otherwise you are just opening the door to dangerous sectlike activity, for example. You have to know exactly what you are looking for and be really clear about your mental state. [Silence.]

You take it, Jeremy!

JEREMY: I am thinking, listening to you, about why people undergo this kind of experience. It seems almost obvious. You said: "Urban life is mysterious in itself. And therefore, where do we come from?" So we can take a plane and see these ancient cultures, like a form of time travel.

We know that during the Cro-Magnon era, these states of altered consciousness took place in the caves of the Dordogne. Trance is something that is very deeply human, and we are drawn to it like camels to water, and have been for an extremely long time, in all cultures.

Now we find ourselves in a world that wants everything to be technological and industrial, where nature has been desanctified, where plants are all but absent, where animals are mainly found in butcher shops or in the zoo. And yes, we do want to go into the recesses of our mind. We want to go into a trance state. It is good for us; it reconnects us with the most deeply human part of our being, the ability we have to transform that the shamans employ. This is a profoundly human characteristic. Shamans say that when they are in trance they are able to transform into animals, precisely.

What is the difference between humans and animals? It is that humans, in their visions, transform into jaguars, but, as far as we know, jaguars do not transform into humans in theirs.

VINCENT: How can we know that for sure?

JEREMY: We cannot be sure. But this is what the shamans who claim they communicate with jaguars say.

VINCENT: These journeys have been a learning experience for me by forcing me to face up to my own stupidity and idiocy. To face up to my own self-importance, in fact. Because, no matter how strong the experience is, and I think shamans experience what they do very strongly, it is impossible for them to know if their experience is the whole of experience. Perhaps the jaguar is lying to them; how can they know?

JEREMY: You're right. . . .

VINCENT: Let's accept that that level of consciousness exists, but that there's another slightly higher level: consciousness. At this level, a person will think he knows everything. This may seem obvious, but it is something that as a human being I know can be very quickly forgotten. A person just has to gain access to a new level of consciousness to think that this level of consciousness encompasses all experience.

There are so many facets to what we can call consciousness, that it is very difficult to know what the truth is. What I took home from this was an extremely strong notion of relativity.

Another thing about the Shipibo shamanic system is man's superiority. Man is at the center of this system and should be an intercessor. Man can communicate with the spirits, and if he is a shaman for a warrior people, he has to master the spirits he deals with. I'm not saying he has to get the upper hand by force, but let's say he has to be stronger, he has to be able to negotiate with this spirit. So, a shaman's never going to let the jaguar take possession of him; that would make him a mediocre shaman. But we really know nothing about it. Perhaps the jaguar is really capable of doing it. . . .

JEREMY: Let's leave the jaguars to their own visions, but getting back to this ability to harness the imagination you mentioned . . . Imagination is, all the same, something that is profoundly human. We don't know how jaguars imagine, but we humans are creatures of language, of symbols. We try to create meaning, and to do this we use the imagination when at the peak of our art—our ability to have images in fact—and shamanism is a set of techniques to stimulate internal imagery.

VINCENT: Absolutely.

JEREMY: So when people in the concrete urban world are drawn to going back to their origins, the tropical forests, the shamans, ancient cultures, substances that induce trance and activate the imagination, like humans have been doing for thirty or forty thousand years, it is no cause for surprise, all things considered.

[Silence.]

JAN: I would like to return to an earlier point, when you were talking about messianism. . . . I would say that is one of the first dangers.

I remember Benny Shanon speaking at a conference on ayahuasca in Amsterdam, two or three years ago. He is a specialist. He is a professor of cognitive psychology at the University of Jerusalem, and he wrote a book published by Oxford University Press about ayahuasca that said he had taken it and based his work on it.

He began his lecture saying: "The first time I took ayahuasca . . . I came back to Jerusalem like a new messiah, I was so sure." And the entire room burst out laughing because everyone there who had ever tried ayahuasca, whether because of its strong visions or a strong relationship, could grasp this experience.

As Westerners, we are fairly primitive when it comes to these tools. You are going to have an experience of healing and rebalancing. The shaman helps us experience mysterious things and these experiences are very beautiful and intense. Then the next morning after it is over we tell ourselves: "So much knowledge! I am just a little turd and I was able to see that, it's wonderful!" You hardly even dare step on the grass.

Two days later the ego has taken over and tells itself: "If I could see that, I am a shaman, I am one of the elect." The mechanism of the ego inside the mind (which is like a child because our culture does not educate it) will gently seize hold of the experience and pull the individual in a direction that is diametrically opposed to the experience itself, for example, like believing you are superior because you possess rare knowledge.

This is a basic, almost mechanical phenomenon that is as simple as gravity. Someone takes ayahuasca and at a given moment, if his experience is strong, as simple as the fact that if someone drops an object that object will fall, he will either take himself for a great shaman or as one of the gods' chosen ones.

This is going to drag him into the twists and turns of an unhealthy reaction, because he is really out of it when it comes to who he thinks he is. This is one of my first pieces of advice: if, at any time, you think you are someone exceptional because you have undergone an experience that is not listed in your cultural directory . . . well then, you should approach it as an adult psychological relationship, which means don't cling to it and avoid imitating or conceptualizing it. Simply hold on to the memory of a new, intense feeling.

That's what I've experienced.

VINCENT: Yes.

JAN: I believed I had to be a great shaman because during my first ayahuasca experiences I had extremely powerful and very clear interactions, and this screwed me up for months and months, until at one time I abandoned any idea or desire related to shamanism.

There is fairly strong collateral psychological damage for people emerging from our culture. This is not the fault of the plant or the healer; it is the result of our lack of education. I don't know if this has been the case for you personally, or if you have seen people like that, somewhat spaced out . . .

VINCENT: This brings me back to intention, and common sense. There are people I've taken ayahuasca with who I've told would be better off taking philosophy courses at the Sorbonne instead! [Laughs.]

I've met extremely intelligent and competent practitioners in other domains than ayahuasca, and they were not showing off. This shows that we have to pay attention . . . to behaving normally.

JEREMY: "Normally"?

VINCENT: We can start digging in to the epistemology of every word— but all I'm saying is simply hold on to your common sense. I am very sensitive about this issue.

I occasionally lost that common sense—because what I was experiencing was too strong and I was not able to find my bearings in reality again. It was more the difficulty of getting a handle on what I had experienced. And finally, it is also what allowed me to recover my balance and stay modest or correct in this dimension.

I believe that if we've been given bodies, spirits with minds, an intelligence that is, well, very reduced but an intelligence all the same, it is so we can use them.

And if you have a strong experience like this, whether it is mystical, from meditation, or even stronger—if you are experiencing it in this body and psyche, it is because there is a reason. So, this body and psyche have to follow it. Me, I stand by my body and my small mind, because . . . that's the way I'm made.

TIGRANE: Wouldn't you say that hasty verbalization is one of the primary dangers lying in wait for everyone coming out of a shamanic experience?

JAN: It's not verbalization; it is the conceptualization of the experience you just had. Integrating this experience is, for example, discovering over time that parts of your behavior have changed. But not: now I can imitate the cosmos.

Once you start falling back into imitation or conceptualization, things start going wrong; in other words, you are trying to cage things that cannot be caged.

It is normal to try, that's how we've been taught. . . .

JEREMY: When I wrote *The Cosmic Serpent,* while I was doing my research, there was a very specific moment when I told myself: "There might be a correspondence between these spirits the shamans are talking about and the molecules of DNA."

For about two weeks, it was just an idea like that, for fun. And when I began seeing, as I reported in my book, so many correspondences, and the further it went, the more clear it seemed there was something to it—it was not just a trippy idea—it precipitated me into a feverish mental space that lasted six weeks at least, and was somewhat messianic. This was a painful time for everyone around me. I talked about nothing else; I thought I had made one of the greatest discoveries of all time.

All at once I had become the center of the world. And perhaps I needed this somewhat grandiose, and may I say messianic, side, in order to dare think this impossible thing. I was listening then to The Cure's "To Wish Impossible Things." And yes, I was hoping for an interface between shamanism and rationalism, which seemed a priori impossible.

So that this idea could be born and travel through me, well, I had to contort myself for a long time. [Grunts of effort.] "I am the new messiah, in my office."

My wife was alarmed and so were my friends.

They were right, in fact. The people around me played their role, just like the shaman's community vigilantly keeps watch on him. The community that tells us: "People are worried."

They also said: "He is exhausting us. He talks about nothing else. We can no longer talk about ordinary things. . . ."

Then, me: "I get the message. I'll shut up and put it into writing. In fact, you motivate me."

And then after a long digestion—the writing itself—I asked myself how I should accompany the book out into the world. On reflection, it was clear that as the author, I had to be antimessianic.

Having gone through an exalted phase, it is next necessary to distance yourself and realize that the more low-key, the more low-profile, the more humble your presentation, the better it will be.

But a little exaltation in the process is probably necessary. To be too normal, to have too much common sense, no: you have to brave vertigo, dare the great leap into the void, and say: "I dare contradict the entire world."

VINCENT: You are completely right. What is important is always the same thing: the result. Is it something good, is it something positive?

Personally I had no messianic impulse for the good reason that ayahuasca already had its messiah: Jeremy. [Laughs.] True, I did not see a whole lot I could add. And when I wrote the book on iboga, at the time I was having the experience and at the time I was writing the book, I was extremely dubious about the experience. I had not yet integrated it very well. Even now, although it's been integrated, it seems so complicated to me and hard to do—but this is something I think we will revisit later—I don't think there is a messianic side, but rather a press agent side. . . . [Laughs.]

JEREMY: The messiah's press agent!

JAN: It is true we have one advantage. We have the ability to communicate, so we can share it. The intense inner questioning triggered by these experiences allowed us to communicate our state of madness, our messianic state of madness. Through communication, you put it in relation to society. And so you can find your place again.

Making these films allowed me to reenter my culture, to settle things down, to expel an internal pressure, to make it so that I no longer talk about shamanism today, except when we see each other or I'm in a debate. But when I'm having a drink with my friends, I don't think about it or talk about it.

We have the enormous good fortune to be individuals that have been able to build bridges between this phenomenon and our culture. This was a thought that came to me quite early. I told myself: "If I've spent fifteen years learning to make movies, used up all my energy learning how to edit one shot into the next, how to work with complex material . . ."

This is not science, but it is still necessary to put its vital energy into things that sometimes come from a really bad scene, with lots of psychological pressures, etc. And once I mastered this tool, finally mastered . . . once I had achieved a certain relationship with the tool that allowed me to make a film, therefore to be considered a filmmaker by my culture, and then go experience shamanism, suddenly I said to myself: "It's logical to make this film that brought me to the jungle, since after all I am going to be playing my role, which is to say composing with something that is truly important for me, since I have become an ayahuasquero—weaving it into my professional life, with the way I have of earning a living, etc." Everything took on meaning.

That is why I returned fifteen days later to my producers.

JEREMY: To sum up, it would be: messianism yes, but as a phase, it should not last.

JAN: I think people always go through this phase. The problem is staying in this phase and believing yourself a great shaman. . . . Shamanism is an indigenous thing!

Ayahuasca is one of the biggest creators of false messiahs. So, pay attention to the nature of what you are thinking of the experience in the back of your mind. Is there humility there, is this awareness being made available to the right person. . . ?

JEREMY: There was an idea that I held to heart already at that time. If you want to bring a new understanding and new concepts into the world and be creative—to reflect, for example, on what you know of nature, of human beings, of other cultures—if you want to dare rethink everything, or try to rethink everything, this requires a certain megalomania and a certain humility at the same time. You must use humility to control the megalomania; they are like a kind of brake and accelerator.

JAN: I would say it a little differently. I would say you have to give yourself complete freedom. Ayahuasca has a role in this phenomenon—generally speaking it is what you said about psychotropic substances. Ayahuasca forces us to suddenly perceive the conditioning of the ideas we think are ours but are in fact artifacts implanted by culture, from childhood with your parents, in the end, all these things.

Once you realize this it gives you the authority to rethink everything. The good aspect of this is revolutionarily joyful; and believing you have been invested with a mission, you're the chosen one, is the negative aspect. It leads you as a person to say: "Why shouldn't I screw everything up and my idea be right?" which is something that every individual should do facing his culture.

I have an enormous advantage, as Vincent does, too, compared to you: as artists we have this freedom. The artist is a performer, from the get-go we have this clown side, we are like the king's fool. For me, any work of art that does not challenge the established system has no purpose. If it exists to comfort its culture's system, it is horrible. It should question, inspire questions, and this is easier for art to do because it's expected.

It is much less accepted in science, and it is in this sense that you have to be invested with much greater courage or even unawareness . . . or bursts of awareness!

JEREMY: I think that everyone around this table has just as much courage. . . .

JAN: No, we are artists, it is much easier, honest.

VINCENT: At the same time, the advantage of science is that it's naturally structured. The scientist has access to a system of thought that must ensure that he can land on his feet at any time . . . unless his system explodes into pieces because his experience was so intense.

JAN: I saw the parable you drew, Jeremy, between *The Cosmic Serpent* and your last book on intelligence in nature. Here's someone who has perceived certain things, put together a theory, and at a certain moment said to himself: "All right, if I want to convince anyone, I have to demonstrate, in the manner my culture wants, proof that nature is intelligent. To go looking for major ideas and slowly weave them together, to force the individual to change dramatically when presented with the reality of nature's intelligence. And to be able to return to the indigenous world."

And this kind of work, which is extremely scientific work, and painstaking and relentless like an ant's work, is courageous. And I thought that was very strong.

[Pause.]

THE AYAHUASCA EXPERIENCE

Vincent: The ayahuasca experience can be separated from shamanism. We can take ayahuasca, for example, in an urban setting and have a very strong experience, one not necessarily connected to the ancestral experience of shamanism. The experience of shamanism is quite close to nature, which actually functions with interfaces of spirits; and someone who takes ayahuasca is not necessarily going to encounter, I don't know, the parrot god who will come talk to him in his dreams or the green mouse who drops by to say hello. He is going to see something else. While someone is having the experience in a shamanic setting, one is going to go through its conceptual system.

And you can have very strong shamanic experiences without taking ayahuasca. But it so happens that ayahuasca is a very formidable agent for altering consciousness.

JAN: What is ayahuasca, for you?

VINCENT: Physically, it is a beverage that is quite unpleasant to drink. Now there are different blends, depending on the shamans who brew it. . . .

JEREMY: Would you agree that it is the Concorde of hallucinogens?

VINCENT: Not at all. I am far from having tried everything, but there are people ayahuasca does not affect very strongly. I have seen people take it, it did not really resonate with them. The experience is different depending on the psychotropic "consciousness opener" that you take. This one has one specific feature; afterward, how to define it . . .

JEREMY: All right, I will give it a shot all the same, if we are going to discuss the experience it induces.

When I experimented with it for the first time, when I was twenty-five, I already had had some experiences with hemp, psylocibin mushrooms, and LSD under my belt. I thought I knew a little about these kinds of things, and my ayahuasca experience stupefied me with the strength, power, and depth in its imagery.

It was flat-out large fluorescent flows, three-dimensional images with a distinctly hallucinatory consistency even though LSD is reputed to be the strongest hallucinogen, and molecularly speaking that is true: all it takes is one hundred millionth of a gram and the parameters of consciousness are altered.

LSD provides distortions, amplifies colors, changes music, but as a rule having real hallucinations with LSD is hard. The same thing with psilocybin, too, which is in the molecular family of DMT: it is interesting, you hear voices or get ideas in your head, but you rarely see things you have never seen before in your life. Scientists have confirmed, moreover, that DMT, one of the active molecules in the ayahuasca brew, is a spectacularly visual hallucinogen.

VINCENT: It's true it is very spectacular.

JEREMY: The advantage of ayahuasca, for the images, over just DMT is that ayahuasca lasts several hours. And what's more, something that is unsettling with regard to other hallucinogens—and I am including alcohol—is that you remain lucid inside, an observer. The anthropologist taking notes can be inside a maelstrom of visual hallucinations. It is as if it was a film at the movies, a horror film or science-fiction movie, you're saying: "Wow, what a film!"

VINCENT: Finally . . . the effect is sometimes so strong . . . this has happened to me, I think to you, too . . . that you have difficulty moving.

JEREMY: You cannot even take notes anymore.

JAN: People often speak of DMT, but the vine itself, the ayahuasca, beyond the fact that it can last several hours, does something quite particular: it causes drunkenness.

It is a very specific kind of drunkenness, one that gives the individual a new perception of his body, of his movements in an organic level. It allows him to enter worlds that are more like visions than hallucinations, because they have a kind of consistency. It is not a distortion of reality, it is an entire other reality that is superimposed over reality, which remains reality. Inside this reality, ayahuasca triggers a drunkenness that makes the subject extremely sensitive emotionally. Among the Ashaninca, there are rituals in which they first drink an ayahuasca brew without DMT. This causes them to cry and lets them encounter their deepest feelings.

With ayahuasca, you are in the presence of a combination that allows you to see and feel at the same time, to simultaneously offer the mind a trip and a perception of the body's organic nature. For me this is one of the specific features of the vine: it authorizes the DMT to move into the bloodstream and to be active, but, overall, it causes this drunkenness that is a state of particular sensitivity. . . .

VINCENT: . . . which is connected to the emotions, for you?

JAN: . . . which is connected to feelings, emotions, but which makes you go aaahhhh. . . ! It is not the DMT that produces the intoxication.

JEREMY: I agree with you again with the words that people use in the Peruvian Amazon. Regarding the drunkenness, you are asked, once you have been administered the ayahuasca: "Estás mareado?" "Are you nauseous?" This is something that specifically affects the stomach. In the meantime, science tells us that the brain, which is in the skull, is connected to one hundred million neurons that constitute the autonomous nervous system. In fact, the brain goes from the solar plexus up into the skull, and it so happens that ayahuasca begins by affecting the stomach and everything that goes with it.

In our culture, nausea is a negative thing: for the indigenous people, it is the heart of the matter. They say, and my experience confirms it, that the visions are strongest while you are vomiting, just before and just after you vomit. This implies that when the nausea increases, the intensity of the visions increases with it.

VINCENT: I have to say that I don't follow you here.

JEREMY: . . . And the people are very clear about the fact that it is a purge, which is what they call it, the *purga*.

Before it gives you movies in your head, it cleanses you. It literally makes you crap, but that is what it is meant to do. Amazonian medicine works with purges. And in a purged body, the animal neocortex can imagine all kinds of worlds.

TIGRANE: Isn't it true that when you purge, whether by the mouth or anus, there is an image of letting go in which you jettison your garbage. You turn inside out so you can take off with less weight. . . .

JAN: I would say that one thing I've learned is that you really need to concentrate on your perception of your stomach, your intestines, so that they relax. You start off feeling like a pile of organs. Next, plunge in to a relaxed state that will carry you through this nausea, and how feeling sick scares you. It's a question of practice. And I would say, after seven years of practice, that ayahuasca has helped me to perceive my mind-organ relationship in a new way.

I did an experiment one day. I wanted to learn just how far one could refine the perception of the experience on the body, so I took ayahuasca and went into a sensory deprivation tank. Incidentally, the thought quickly came to me, after about ten minutes, that this was a very bad idea, because it intensified the strength of the experience. But the Indians teach you how to get through all these states, even states that are quite strong. Also I have several hours of astral journeying behind me, so I got through the thing. But because of it I was able to observe my organs in an enhanced way. When you are floating in a sensory deprivation tank, you are obliged to relax your body. You no longer know which side is up, which side is down, you are floating in the void.

VINCENT: You did this where?

JAN: It doesn't really matter; I did it in a tank. . . . I will tell you someday what country I went to to do this. But by forcing me to be completely relaxed this allowed me to realize: "What is this gigantic train I am hearing? It is the roar of my arteries beating at their normal rhythm. What is that terrible noise? It's my organs rumbling because of the vine, which is making me aware of them. . . ." I felt the blood flowing through my veins.

I helped myself, singing the songs of traditional shamans to help me make the journey, I truly entered that world, and I often talk about it because it is a tool of self-discovery. It is also feeling the arrival of fear. Ayahuasca is going to make you feel fears that come from far away. The shaman will guide you to pull yourself out at just the right moment, in any case that's my experience, but once you have something that is not working in your life, you will feel the warning sign of fear, your body will have a new attitude because it has been educated by the healers that way.

And I think that one of the things that shamans do is keep their bodies completely relaxed during the time they have terrible nausea, so that their physical well-being can guide the mind into a territory of well-being; and they project this well-being toward others. . . .

VINCENT: It's a profession.

JAN: It is a profession: to feel well, tranquil, poised while you are turned upside down physically and psychologically. Often shamans have told me: "First make yourself comfortable, then think of the person you are treating with good and beautiful thoughts."

One may think that these are simple things, but it is quite complicated because when a plant strips you bare, it strips bare your fears, your fantasies, your terrors. It forces you to encounter the feeling of death; even if it is virtual, your mind is still going to perceive it. It is going to perceive the mortal organic mechanism, which is going to be unplugged one day, scaring you even more. Learning to cross through these stages in order to live more intensely appears to be one of the shaman's, the healer's, modes of operation.

VINCENT: While we are on this subject, it should be pointed out that a shaman who is guiding a ceremony often takes less ayahuasca than the people participating in it.

JAN: Not necessarily. I am only familiar with Shipibo-Conibo shamanism, so I can only speak of a very limited branch of the practice. I would say that actually the shaman sometimes takes a little less, but you must realize that he takes it every day so he is saturated. The transition between his natural state during the day and his state during the session is less significant.

VINCENT: Quite so; but he doesn't necessarily take a quart of ayahuasca before guiding a session.

JAN: In any case, I have seen Shipibo shamans take quite substantial doses, the equivalent of a whole glass of extremely strong plants, for specific moments.

VINCENT: And perform?

JAN: Yes, I even believe that in the session that can be seen at the end of *D'autres mondes* [Other Worlds], where, incidentally, I am laid out on the floor, it is also quite intense for them. I can see it by looking at the images.

So, I've seen both cases. It's true that if they want to get up and do things, they may take less. But the notion of quantity is a surprising thing.

I was in Peru several weeks ago. Out of five sessions, I was arriving at the fourth, and when the *curandero* entered the room, all at once I felt my intoxication increase. I felt it was going to be quite strong. I knew it was going to be an important session. I knew that, whatever quantity I took, this session was going to be the strongest even though the previous evening I had taken twice as much, and the next day I would take twice as much again. And the session was quite strong.

I think that the shaman is capable of inducing an experience in you through his own power independently of the plant.

VINCENT: That's obvious. But we are getting into an explanation of processes that are hard to put into words because we do not know all the inner workings. And even if we knew all the inner workings, I do not think it would say much to many people.

It is obvious that shamans have a "technical skill" that goes beyond the taking of psychotropic substances; otherwise just anybody could be a shaman. Certainly shamans, wherever they live, truly possess a know-how that would appear like magic, if we could really see it.

JAN: What is magic?

VINCENT: Just like when you showed up fifty years ago with a walkie-talkie, it was magic.

JAN: Exactly.

VINCENT: It is an exchange of knowledge, of representations of the world and actions on the world, that are actually quite different. But this is something that is very difficult for a Westerner who has not experienced them a fortiori to imagine.

Afterward, in order to really understand these mechanisms, it is like everything else: you have to practice. . . .

For me, what is quite interesting is that I have been initiated into different traditions from around the world. There are things that are similar and things that are different, but by paying close attention you can see a little of what makes them tick. . . .

JAN: Do you mean the bridges?

VINCENT: No, the way in which a shaman is going to proceed. The first time this happens you say to yourself: "God damn, this guy is super terrific." And then you go to another region of the world, the same sort of hocus-pocus is performed on you, and you say to yourself: "This is super terrific; but he is not doing this by chance, is he?" And the next time, you tell yourself: "This is good; I've had this done to me already." Because of this, you are able to progress because you understand better what appeared to you. You say: "Okay, you can move on to the next thing."

This is what our era today allows. Before, when someone was confronted by a body of knowledge, there was only that body of knowledge. It is this intersection of experiences that is really inspiring.

So, getting back to how I see ayahuasca, I see it as a technical skill—but not the only one. It is for this reason that I put so much stress on warning labels.

The more a person has an experience like ayahuasca, or other psychotropic plants, the more it opens consciousness, so it is going to let things appear to someone who may be completely close-minded.

For example, I practiced Zen for ten years with truly great diligence, trying to do it every day. At the time, I experienced great difficulty understanding just what I was up to, but I was really unrelenting, and this had two effects. The first is that when I took ayahuasca, I was much more ready and receptive.

And then when I did Zen again, I said to myself, "Hold on, I am finally doing Zen!" I was not under the influence of ayahuasca, but ayahuasca had turned me on to an energetic sensitivity that made me much more sensitive to Zen. And, paradoxically, Zen made it possible for me to integrate ayahuasca, because all those times I'd spent sitting in a lotus position trying to let my thoughts flow by like clouds in the sky, which is one of the things of Zen, well anyway when I found myself confronting experiences that were extremely intense psychologically, this was something that helped me quite a bit. But I digress. . . .

JEREMY: No, that's a beautiful story.

VINCENT: So, to finish, this kind of experience can be extremely tempting but also quite destabilizing. There are people involved in all kinds of traditions based on awakening who think to themselves: "I am going to take ayahuasca." This can be a good thing or a bad thing; it all depends on what you have grasped and what kind of beating you can take.

What you say is very important: a shaman is going to enable you to have the most powerful experience possible telling you that when it is over, if you are not dead, you will be stronger. Even if you stumble upon a cool shaman who is open to Westerners, after a minute he will ask you: "Are you really going to go there or not? If you don't want to go then what the hell are you doing here?" Basically, for someone who has it together and is truly courageous, it is an extraordinary experience.

But someone who is a little weak or fragile, or has problems, who has read an article and said to himself: "Hey, I am going to take that, this is going to be a spiritual revolution, we shall get healing," unfortunately risks, unless he has skilled guidance, stumbling into something that can really hurt him, and this is a point I really think needs to be stressed.

JEREMY: Do you have specific cases that you can talk about, people who have been completely turned upside down by ayahuasca, datura . . . ?

VINCENT: Or iboga. Listen, I don't know about "completely messed up" because they were not too stable to begin with, but I am not sure the experience did them any good.

JEREMY: That's easy to believe, but do you know—because we have all crossed paths with a certain number of people—of a case involving anyone who would have been perfectly normal, his head on straight, who all at once fell into pieces because of an ayahuasca experience? I, personally, don't know of anyone. On the other hand, people who have been messed up . . .

For example, I know someone in Switzerland who got himself invited to a session; he did not even know what it was—he thought it was like smoking a joint. He told himself: "Great, people are getting together in an Alpine chalet, everyone drinks this brew that is somewhat disgusting, and then everyone is really flying!" Except what he experienced was his own death. He saw the limits of his own worldview. Afterward he was very unhappy. He said: "My way of looking at the world was completely altered and no one warned me!" For a year or two he was quite bad off. You see, this was not written on the package. . . . It would be good if it were written on the package, but, unfortunately, because of the illegality of the thing, it can't be. But let's not get into that question now.

So, yes, it is something extremely powerful. Yes, it helps alter the way you look at the world. So, you have to be an imbecile or very ill informed to take ayahuasca. . . .

JAN: . . . for kicks.

VINCENT: Let me ask you the same question this way: Do you know lots of people who are balanced, with their heads on straight and everything?

JEREMY: I am going to have the audacity to say, for the benefit of our conversation, that I think my head is on straight.

And then I love numbers, understanding things. I need things to be solid. I am not interested in believing; I want to know.

So, let's say that I have done around one ayahuasca session a year, for twenty years. A good session gives me enough material to work on for twelve months. The eleven months of the year in Western reality is the time when I download the experience and try to honor it.

JAN: To integrate it then . . .

JEREMY: To integrate it, to put what I've learned into practice, to test all of it to better develop the question I want to pose for the next session. And besides, if your behavior is morally correct with the people around you during these twelve months, when you show up the next time, the spirit of ayahuasca is going to kick your butt a lot less than if you had been a liar and a manipulator. So, it is a kind of life ethic.

VINCENT: That's not something I can talk about because I am neither a liar nor a manipulator. [Laughs.] True, everyone has their own problems, but those are not some of mine.

JEREMY: I try to never lie. It is true that everyone has their own problems. But the fact remains that ayahuasca has a tendency to confront you with your problems first thing, straight off, before getting into the matter. You want to get answers about DNA, but first you have to see how big an idiot you are. This is all part of the purge.

Another thing, in my opinion ayahuasca stimulates that part of the brain where you feel fear. You are there, you are scared, you don't know what you are scared of, but you realize that you are scared and you can even be scared of the fear you are feeling. . . . In the beginning, often for the first hour, it is a fairly animal-like feeling.

JAN: I think it is connected to the fact that you are beginning to perceive yourself as an organic entity. You are so much in the habit of the mind controlling the body that when all at once the body takes back its rights, your mind dissolves into a maelstrom of emotions and organs, and you perceive yourself as an organic entity. So, it is knowledge. Except that the first stage you face is terror. . . . That's why it is necessary to be relaxed.

JEREMY: What you just said reminded me of what some neuroscientists say—namely, that hallucinogens function by short-circuiting our neocortex with which we reason, which allows other layers of the brain, as well as the body itself, to gain the upper hand.

It is as if the neocortex had to go take a seat in the back, and suddenly the one at the wheel is the body.

JAN: There are so many unknowns. . . .

JEREMY: . . . and in fact, it is intelligent. You recognize yourself—it is not your reasonable self—and you are almost surprised to see another intelligence inside of you. All at once, you can smell the odor of people. People you know seem bizarre to you. You have never seen them like this, and your body tells you things about them. . . . This can be scary. At the same time I find that going through the experience, preferably several times, and reconnecting with your animal being, provides certain advantages.

JAN: To borrow your example, which I find quite judicious: you are used to being in the driver's seat, and you suddenly find yourself in the back of your own jalopy with someone else at the wheel, someone you have never seen driving; so you are terrified. Until you discover that if you pull his arms off the steering wheel, things turn sour. Little by little you realize that he is quite a good driver in fact. What's more, you are on a road you've never taken and he knows how to drive along this road, whereas if you were at the wheel, you would be steering with your thoughts and drive straight into a wall.

JEREMY: So you shut up and watch! [Laughs.]

JAN: That's it! You learn how to tell yourself: "Leave it alone. . . . Take it easy; stay calm."

JEREMY: In any case, the Amazonian shamans I know, if you ask their advice about how to be during a session, they say: "Stay quiet, don't disturb the others. You try to stay sitting up rather than lying down, and you watch. You confront the visions. This will last four to five hours, but you try to stay calm."

JAN: It's fairly astonishing, this kind of tense relaxation—you are relaxed physically but vigilant mentally.

So, don't grab, but stay alert, because, as you say, this is a warrior's art. A commando operation: neutralize the ego and your fears, by letting them dissolve with each breath in order to allow the body, or the self, to emerge.

These are sensations people rarely experience. Perhaps athletes, at a given moment, or those people who have to be simultaneously completely tensed and relaxed in order to be on target, to make certain decisions?

JEREMY: Like skiers before their descent, who run the film of their course in their minds, with their eyes closed?

VINCENT: They are no longer thinking when they do it.

JEREMY: . . . that's it, so they can let go completely.

[Silence.]

But there are still technical issues. How do you tell the difference between a projection and a vision? In other words, okay, you are a Westerner, your parents did not teach you how to hallucinate, and there you are, hallucinating, and it's completely astonishing, you are seeing all sorts of things, they are right there before your eyes, you are almost weeping, it is too beautiful, you tell yourself: "Yeah, this is the hidden Truth with a capital T."

But is what you are seeing truly things that are real and sacred, or are you simply projecting?

VINCENT: An example?

JEREMY: An example. Some ecologists who go to the Amazon and drink ayahuasca have a tendency to see: "Nature is weeping. Gaia spoke to me, the planet is asking for help. So I am going to use this experience to motivate my ecologist approach." And there is, precisely, a messianic side to this: "The planet needs me, I have to save it."

Personally I do not perceive this message. What life tells me through ayahuasca is, "I am incredibly strong, I diversify myself, I don't give a hoot about what you say, I am inside your body. Watch this movie!"

It is anthropocentricism to think that we are endangering the planet. It is a very grave thought. In fact, we are endangering ourselves—right, yes, that's my opinion. Still the fact remains that we have people like this who go within and capture their own ecological guilt, perhaps? Is the planet truly crying, or are they simply projecting their guilt?

VINCENT: That's a very good question. I believe that both are right. What these experiences open up is precisely the multiple and complex nature of consciousness. I think that in this kind of experience, every layer is in play.

In the case of the ecologist, it resonates with his own way of seeing the world, and it also resonates with a reality. So, that is what will vibrate inside of him. And for him it is absolutely true, for it is a reality in any event. You, meanwhile, have a different conceptual diagram, and that will cause something else to resonate inside. This kind of experience makes it possible to see the diversity of the universe: we are on a very small planet, in a very small galaxy, and we have this kind of extremely concentrated thing that makes each one of us see things in a necessarily egocentric manner, through one's own prism.

So, I believe that all experiences are true, and they are all correct. Now, you are asking a question that is valid for ayahuasca and for other psychotropic substances. I think that there are different technical features, features that will cause you to see different types of visions. I talked about this in the book on iboga because with iboga you have visions that materialize before your eyes, when your eyes are open. It is different with ayahuasca. You have visions that come from inside your brain. And even inside your brain you have visions that come in a different way. You have some that can pop up behind your eyelids, you have some that can show up—I don't know if this happens to you—at different spots on your mental screen.

I think there are things that are projections of your subconscious, things that are projections of your unconscious, and things that your own mind mixes together. Then there are the visions inspired by the shaman; there are things that are created by the people sharing the experience with you, that are the synthesis of a shared experience of consciousness and that inspire a certain kind of energy; and this energy will materialize within each person through a different vision, but that can also be an imagistic synthesis, in the same way that an advertising image will synthesize the intention and desire of the announcer so that it resonates with the desire of the consumer. It is the same principle.

All this is quite hard to take for a Westerner who is not used to finding himself inside all this. It can also be memory, because we have a very substantial collective memory.

Depending on the place you are at, depending on the people with whom you are taking it, depending on your own cellular, psychological, historical memory, depending upon everything you have experienced and inherited, ayahuasca—and iboga even more so, which is really going to hunt down what's buried deepest inside you—is going to project in front of you or in your mind memory phenomena that are not necessarily your own memories but that are the substance from which you are woven, in the same way that molecularly, and even atomically, a person is woven from . . . what's the expression, "star dust"?

JAN: Our atoms are as old as the universe. "We are star dust" is the poetic way of expressing it.

VINCENT: All of these things have the power to resonate; and a shaman is capable of making them echo inside you.

JAN: What the Shipibo shamans say about this is that there are two visions, and for me it is fairly clear: there is the true vision and then, right next to it, is the vision that comes from the imagination.

I can say truthfully that very few of my visions have come from my imagination. One day I saw an amphitheater like the National Assembly building filled with toasters. I asked myself: What's the story here? and then the vision vanished. [Laughs.]

Once I saw a hyperrealistic pizza deliveryman, but I attributed it to my nonshamanic imagination. And recently—this is pretty funny—because I had just finished shooting *99 Francs,* so I'd been spending time with Jean Dujardin, who was on the set every day; we shot the film in Venezuela and from there I dashed off to the Amazon.

Shooting a film activates your mind, the way you think. In my case, I drop the reins when I make a film so I can be in a kind of instinctive and creative mental space. The horses are going at a full gallop. I only make sure that they take the right path. I don't know if this is the right method, but up to now it is the only one I have.

So, after shooting this film, which took over three months, I was back in the Amazon. I took ayahuasca, and all at once I was confronted by visions of Indians in canoes, groups of Indians, a mythological vision, a little like the boats that form parades on the Nile; and it is hard to see things clearly. My mind was racing—with tons of thoughts; it was hard to concentrate. Then a canoe passed by and I saw Jean in it, dressed like he was in the film surrounded by Indians, and he waved to me. I laughed and told myself: "I am not in tune with the plant. My imagination, my memory are all active at the same time; the waves are scrambled." It made me laugh.

This first session was like a cleansing. During the second hour, fortunately, I went back to purely shamanic visions, which have a real consistency, one that extends back years.

When a vision occurs, it awakens the memory of previous visions that I thought I had forgotten. I remember that I have visited this world before although I had forgotten it in my ordinary consciousness. Let's say that I am getting back to a place where I recognize myself—in a vision that has a meaning that I seem to clearly get and have gotten for years, and which weaves a higher level of the experience.

And I wanted to cite two examples connected to things I have experienced.

The first is an experience that I had several years ago now but that I remember clearly. I had begun the ceremony in a fragile state after several successive days of ceremony. At the start of the ceremony, the song begins. It is a warrior song, a cold and muted song that does not vibrate in the area of emotional sensitivity. Through the plant and the shaman I seemed to be receiving the message to supervise my thoughts and not cling to the experience. I concentrate and accept it inside by promising to keep watch during the session upon the ungraspable aspect of the experience. Once I make this promise, the song grows louder, everything becomes ultrasensitive, my visions flood in and penetrate the light.

It is always terrible when you see a vision described or when you recount it because you say that's all there is, the other is gone. . . . But I would describe it as a kind of vision of light and eternity (that's all!). That's when I, who had just made an agreement not to cling, five minutes earlier—the deep serious-minded agreement of an ayahuasquero with his practice, not to cling—opened my two arms, welcomed the light, and had this thought: "I am immortal, yes, thank you, I see it now."

Just then the shaman's song changed completely. There was almost a kind of inner snickering that froze me with fright and which went "han-nan-nan-nan-nan-nan," and I realized that I had clutched the information that I was having a vision, a feeling, and had immediately transformed this into an incorrect thought. Perhaps I was in touch with the undying essence inside, the vital energy, the soul; but in this instance, it was the organic creature I am and who thinks it is going to die one day. So, keep vigilance over one's thoughts.

There is another experience of the same kind, connected to the notion of "You are having the experience; what will you bring back from the experience?" So, I did another session—the one that was filmed in *Other Worlds,* which was quite lively—and at one moment I had the impression that the shaman was weaving something around my thought in his song.

It is extremely subjective, but it appeared clear to me, and then I heard an inner voice telling me, "Do not trust thought" that became wed to the song. I agreed to this wholeheartedly, and then I realized with a shock at a deeper level: "This is still thought. . . . Not trusting a thought remains a thought." And then I literally went into a tailspin because I could no longer trust anything, because I am a creature who thinks. So I took refuge in the sensation of the body.

VINCENT: I agree and I think you have put your finger on the problems this can pose for a Westerner, who relies on another kind of conceptual system. He should be capable of making the mix exactly in the way you just described it; the psyche is not organized in the same manner at all. I think we have mental compartments that the Shipibo do not have and vice versa. When I mentioned danger earlier, this was what I meant.

JEREMY: I find that when dealing with matters that are hard to conceive, metaphors make fine thinking tools, so I am going to suggest one or two, and then we can discuss them.

The ayahuasca experience is like being in a car accident. In the sense that it is an experience that is close to death, or in any case an experience where people can easily feel death. Furthermore, it is a common theme in ayahuasca shamanism; and the etymology of the word *ayahuasca* is "vine of the dead" or "vine of souls."

Like a car accident, it is fairly dramatic and you can see your life passing before your eyes. And then you are shocked, you are ill, you are dazed; you have been through somersaults; your stomach feels upside down. Except that, continuing with what you said, this lasts three hours rather than three seconds.

A car accident happens quickly. In ayahuasca it is as if everything is in slow motion and you are dreaming, with lots of things going on, except you have the time to observe them. Personally, I find this to be a job, let's say, of devotion. If you want to explore these altered states of consciousness, it is, like Benny Shanon says, a kind of unexplored continent for us; and for the first people there it involves taking notes and coming back with maps.

So here I get to something very concrete that helps me during my ayahuasca experiences. When I am in the maelstrom of visions, the goal is—while looking, while feeling—to understand things if things are being communicated to me and quickly note them down with a felt-tip pen in the dark, in a small notebook, a little like an intrepid reporter among Indians; and then, it is almost an art, writing in the dark, when you are—

JAN: I don't know how you do it! [Laughs.]

JEREMY: It is pretty funny; the next day you have a bunch of hieroglyphs that you have to decipher. "What was I trying to say there?" They are often a kind of coded message, because you are already in a state that is almost outside language. But I make the effort of finding the words. If something seems important to me, I stop watching the movie to quickly jot down some words to have a chance of remembering it the next day. That is the work, coming back from over there with information on the questions I've asked myself. And I think it quite simply helps to have a little notebook next to you and a goal. You begin the session with a question, you look for a piece of information, you are at the service of this little search, you are going to get slapped down, and in the meantime you keep your eyes open, and if you understand something, you note it down; and then, just like that, you live your experience.

JAN: It is strange because we have completely different ways of experiencing the trip. I could never take a note; I have the specific impression I have to disconnect, to work to refrain from interpreting . . . so I can go deeper into the experience.

To use your example of a car accident, I am telling myself: "Gee, this guy is strong, if he can take notes when the car is rolling end over end!" [Laughs.] I tell myself that it is part of a giant stunt and that the trick is to be firmly concentrating while the car is rolling over, while hoping to more or less remember what happened.

I believe we all relate to it differently because we are all looking for different things. Even if the things that each of us brings back speak to us all. When I listen to us talking, I think that we are very close but that our methods are completely different.

JEREMY: Concerning memory, I find that these altered states of consciousness have a tendency to be state specific, unique to this state. When you are no longer in that state, you do not recall what you saw. It is like how dreams evaporate in the morning after waking.

JAN: Except when you practice it faithfully, you will almost always find your same dream every night. In the end it is no longer truly a dream but a reality that you are entering, one that will leave you with more information about itself over time.

But I agree with you entirely. There are times when you finish a trip telling yourself: "There, I know a lot," and then when you wake up early in the morning, it has become much more vague, because you have left that state. It is a little like in *City Lights*—except there it is alcohol, and it might not be a good example. But you know, there is an alcoholic who is Charlie Chaplin's friend who only recognizes him when he is smashed. During the day he does not recognize him, but at night their paths cross, and he recognizes him again.

When you go back into this state, it reopens everything you have learned and encountered, all your memories, and all at once this information is available again. It was not lost but temporarily shut away. It is impossible for me to take notes during the ceremony; I am concentrating on relaxing my guts and on the songs.

JEREMY: The importance of the songs of the ayahuasquero shamans is that each species supposedly has a spirit, an essence; and the essence of these essences (which is what you can see in the visions) is to emit a vibration or a melody.

Each species has its own melody. If you wish to know tobacco, you learn the melody of tobacco. This is something that you are taught during the visions; it is the essence of the information that is being communicated to you, from the shamanic point of view. You said earlier the shaman's job is to remember the different melodies: the power of the shaman is gauged on the number of his *icaros,* or shamanic songs.

All this fits into a mnemonic approach in which you go into this other dimension and you come back with a teaching; you bring back the essence of essences, which proves to be a melody, and you use the melody to remind yourself of it. This is the approach of the hunter, who summons the spirits like he would call game by imitating its cry.

There is this relationship in the indigenous notion of ayahuasca. That is how it is practiced, like a hunter in search of information, and with a technique for remembering what you have learned.

VINCENT: That is totally true; that is exactly how it takes place.

JAN: How it really takes place, I don't know. . . .

VINCENT: The truly shamanic technique, in any case, is like that.

JAN: Over the years, I think of moments from ceremonies during which I had very strong experiences when there were no songs, when the shaman did not sing, when the shamans started moving outside the *maloca.*

Of course, if a ceremony begins and the shaman does not sing during the first hour, and not for the first hour and a half, you feel alone, you think you are all alone in any case in that world, you can internally supplicate him to sing so you can . . . bring consistency to the visions. You are going to concentrate immediately on the song and be guided by it.

But at the level of the nature of the experience, the strongest moments I have lived were located in phases that lasted around twenty minutes, between two songs.

VINCENT: I think that you have two things. Shamanic initiation is a very scientific initiation. It is like going to school. Someone tells you: "This is the letter A, this is the letter B. . . ." You have a spirit, this spirit corresponds to a song, which is a vibration. And the shaman is going to repeat it to you as many times as it takes for you to learn it.

JEREMY: It is a university. . . .

VINCENT: It is a tradition, a university. . . . It is codified in this way. And then you have the ayahuasca itself.

The shamanic peoples have not drunk ayahuasca all the time, they had other plants or other methods. This is something I do not think a Westerner can acquire. It takes too much time. Very well, he could have it inside, he could have a memory that is going to awaken, that is going to say: "Ah! I recognize this, this, and this; it's good." Or else, the poor guy, he is going to work like a poor devil because it requires a whole lifetime and more to completely immerse oneself in a culture, to understand how something works, to sing the icaros. It is the same thing as going to church, repeating the Our Father thing, or going to college and learning mathematical formulas by heart; I think that would be just as hard for someone who does not have it inside.

And then there is ayahuasca, and what it is going to provoke . . . there, we are no longer completely with the Indians. You did an initiation with the Ashaninca, who are still quite close, from what I've gathered, to their original culture; in other words, they are still quite close to nature.

When you go, for example, to Guillermo's, he drives a car, he has a telephone, a satellite dish, the TV; there is a new airport in Pucallpa; he has been everywhere in Europe and so his consciousness is no longer the same. But he still takes ayahuasca, which connects him to other things.

And what you say, Jan, about these guys who move about, if I can permit myself this observation, is something else: it is the energy that is functioning differently at those moments. You create an energy field during the session, and this field is adjustable in accordance with the position of the people in it. You have people who sing with ayahuasca; you create an energy field. This is why when someone moves, for example, you can start to vomit. Fine, here we are talking about very technical things, but I think it is easily understandable for people who have done feng shui.

It is the energetic field that is altered at this moment, and with someone who knows how to do it, or who does it at the wrong time, you can experience very bizarre things, because under ayahuasca (and even more if you do it frequently), your energetic body is going to vibrate differently.

JAN: I didn't make myself understood very well. What I wanted to say is that, for me, the shaman starts becoming active, on the strongest level, in a situation that does not include song. This has happened several times with a certain kind of extremely strong vision. It travels from mind to mind.

VINCENT: Yes, absolutely.

JAN: . . . which allows me to simply say that the icaros are the center, but that there are operational modes used by the Shipibo shamans that do not go through the icaros.

VINCENT: That's what I was saying: there can be very different things. You can have the ayahuasca experience without having a shamanic initiation. In ayahuasca, you can have doors that offer access to different things.

I know people who go to the Amazon, who almost live there and truly go through a shamanic initiation. It is a kind of private school and you acquire a particular kind of knowledge, which is related to nature spirits and things like that.

And you have people who go through the ayahuasca experience and have another kind of knowledge, one that is perhaps more universal?

[Pause.]

TOOLS FOR THE TRIP

JAN: I do not know how it works, but frankly guys, I think it is more complicated than learning songs. . . .

VINCENT: We all agree on that. I have never learned the slightest song. But for some people, it is necessary to teach them because it works like school.

JAN: It works like school, but it is not only learning songs. You enter certain modes of vision, you survive inside them, you learn to weave states, visions, with the song. When we say: "You learn songs like in school," it amounts to reconsidering their system with our own.

VINCENT: Of course. You are not forced to have the song system in order to understand something else.

JAN: My point of view is that no one is going to be able to explain how shamanism works. When you talk of the songs by saying it is like college, I would say that there is that element to it, but that the trick to it is still somewhere else. And I do not know what it is—I am not a shaman.

VINCENT: . . . to remain on this postulate that it is an extremely complex reality, so it cannot be reduced to certain things.

JAN: You said it.

VINCENT: It's obvious. On the other hand, the purpose, all the same, is to become more aware, so you can discover a certain way to function. Its purpose is not to make you stupider and stupider every time you go there and never realize anything.

JAN: I have not been saying anything to the contrary!

VINCENT: I think that there is a happy medium between having the impression of knowing everything and having the impression at a given moment of having spotted things, confronting them with one's own experience and forming hypotheses.

JAN: And I will be the first to do so during the course of a conversation.

VINCENT: There are things that I don't know as absolute values, but just simply because I was taught them in that way. When I hear someone explain them to me verbally, I say: "Yes, it is validated by different things; what you are saying there is something a shaman taught me, and not in a verbal form."

You have a reality of the experience, and a vision of the experience. But since we are sitting around a table to talk about them, it is interesting to be able to rationalize them a little.

JAN: Definitely. And in this rationalization, what I would like to say is: it takes place with icaros, and it takes place without them.

In my opinion, something like a great mystery should remain over certain things for us. . . .

VINCENT: Mysteries are made to be . . .

JEREMY: . . . admired? [Laughs.]

VINCENT: Admired, but also . . .

JEREMY: . . . pierced.

JAN: You said earlier, Vincent, we should not forget that shamans are warriors, that when you go there, you are going to get smacked, the guy is going to put your head in the bucket,* and test you. He is going to test you to see if you really want to go there. But I would add a cautionary note to this. There are two possible perspectives. You will be initiated to become a healer, in which case the shaman is going to put your head, your anus, and your whole body in the bucket; but if you are doing this to know yourself and know the medicine and the spirits, you are going to be in for much less of a rough time, you are not going to die inside so violently; in short it is going to be less intense.

---

*[The bucket here refers to the receptacles used in ayahuasca sessions for people to vomit in when purging. —*Trans.*]

And the thing that is still potentially important concerning the people who may possibly read this book, those who may turn to indigenous medicine for healing—"rebalancing" may perhaps be a more appropriate word—they are going establish a balance with their emotions, feelings, nature, and thought, all that, and the shaman is going to go to work inside. I do not think that the shaman's intent at this moment is that of a warrior. If the individual has a lot of suffering that needs to be expelled, he is going to vomit, he is going to be sick, he has to go through all that, but it must be done differently. It has to be gentler for this kind of person.

JEREMY: Something we might add is that in contemporary Amazonian reality, in a number of indigenous societies, the young no longer go through this experience. We are in a world where there is a historical crisscross; indigenous Amazonian youth seem rather obsessed by the urban, technological world and are turning their back on shamanic traditions. In the meantime, us folks from the technological world, in a world bled of meaning but full of objects, well, we are taking almost the exact opposite path. We are going toward their world in search of meaning and going to the roots of their knowledge.

There are some funny things going on because now indigenous youth are realizing that there is a demand on the part of the Westerners; Western interest in shamanism has kept some traditions alive. And shamanism, a source of transformation, is itself in the midst of transforming.

VINCENT: With an economic impetus. It is sure that the Westerners who come and pay fifty dollars a session are a motivation to a young person from Pucallpa.

JAN: When I was in Pucallpa, I saw boat pilots who said they were learning the songs by ear in the evening. They were listening to them to understand them better and learning them so they could reproduce them and invite Westerners to take ayahuasca. It's really a situation here where just anything goes.

But actually, when we arrived with our Western technology in a remote community where there were no opportunities, filming helped the young appreciate the shamans, whereas previously they had not necessarily considered shamans as capable of inspiring their lives. They saw us approaching the elders in the village; it was they who interested us. Meanwhile the young people were thinking that perhaps being initiated could provide a means of survival.

And I would say that if they enter into traditional initiation even for reasons like this, so they can use it commercially later, once they have entered it, it will inevitably take them to the knowledge. A moment comes when you must go there; therefore they will discover things, they are going to become shamans, and if the impulse was given to them because they told themselves it would give them the tools for survival, that's good, as you said, for maintaining a tradition.

It is true that we tend to see the opposite. When arriving in the communities, we see how the young want Nikes and are beginning to own televisions, and it is the end of the world because they don't have the means to own material things; and they rush away from their deep traditions and knowledge and end up with nothing.

So, for me, the goal was actually to get the film distributed into their communities so that the young could see that the scientists of our world, in other words eminent people, were taking an interest in shamanism, that people were talking about it, and that their culture contained important information about it and they had no reason to be ashamed.

In July, I went down into the lower Ucayali—I visited eleven communities in the Ucayali to scout a film I was going to make—and in the lower Ucayali, there were no more curanderos in the villages.

VINCENT: Where is that, the lower Ucayali?

JAN: It is below Pucallpa, after you pass the lagoon. . . . When you go down the lower Ucayali, there are no longer any healers in the villages. The village leader will tell you, a foreigner, on arrival with a certain pride: "Oh no, we no longer have any shamans, any curanderos."

VINCENT: "Don't worry. . . ."

JAN: Exactly, "don't worry." At this moment, you say: "That's really too bad." What's more, you are going to shoot your film in a community that is still lucky enough to have one. Fortunately in the upper Ucayali, from Santa Rosita to all the other communities—that is where I shot the film, in Bethania, Juventus, San Rafael—there were still two to three healers per community.

The movement here is going in the opposite direction. They have been slaughtered and told that it was better not to have a shaman. Their communities have biblical names, New Jerusalem, New Bethania; it is terrible. And the thing that most depressed me in the communities of the lower Ucayali during my last trip is that they wanted to perform songs for me at night. They had a village financed by evangelists where you saw women in traditional Shipibo clothes singing Jesus is coming back in Spanish with a guy playing the organ. . . . Yet three years earlier, in the same community, you had real traditional songs in the Shipibo language.

JEREMY: Missionaries of all stripes have done much to put the idea into the Indians' head that the shaman is devilish and that if they want to be civilized people and, precisely, take part in the shiny technological world, they must abandon these devilries and sorceries.

JAN: *Shamans Through Time,* which you wrote, shows this over the course of history clearly. What is terrible is that this phenomenon is still active; it is not the past.

VINCENT: We have digressed a little. So, in order to return to the very interesting question of how—

JEREMY: Brainstorming on the ABCs of what to know and what to avoid.

VINCENT: I would say that it is necessary to set off with an open mind, but also with a lot of distrust. I am not convinced, truly, that it is necessary to go and have this kind of experience, so . . .

JEREMY: Tigrane said: "Why would a young indigenous person of sixteen want to do this? And why would a sixteen-year-old here want to do this?" He or she would have to be eighteen anyway, but fine. . . .

TIGRANE: When we look at the texts that have been written over the past ten years, what we read about is healing. And when we look at what is brewing or being said today for people who have not had the experience, there is an impression that it is rather like a mystical attraction, perhaps a little naive, a kind of belief or faith. . . .

JAN: It is very different; a young sixteen-year-old Indian has no desire for great mystical revelations. He will go see the shaman when he is not feeling well and cannot go to the hospital. Going to see the healer is really a last resort. Unless he has a problem of a shamanic nature; if he starts feeling like he is under a spell or something like that, then he will go see the shaman to be cured.

Very few seek initiation. In the communities where I filmed *Other Worlds,* I met young people around twenty who said: "When I am thirty, I will take ayahuasca, just for the principle of it." And then there were girls in the crew who had tasted it. But they were surprised all the same; for them ayahuasca was something you turned to when you had a good reason not just because you wanted to get high, to have an experience.

JEREMY: That's totally right.

JAN: And then, they know it is a serious thing, it is etched into their system. What ayahuasca is going to show them is something they know culturally, it's part of their way of understanding reality, nature, the nature spirits. All of this is a concrete reality; you won't find a young Shipibo who doesn't believe in this. There are young people there who have had visions without ever taking ayahuasca; it's in their genes and culture, it's in the power of the places where they live.

I've often seen people who tell me shamanic things when I'm filming. They tell me: "I don't take ayahuasca, but one day I was walking in the jungle and on a tree I saw . . ." Or else: "I got a song from a dream." This is woven into their very lives, so why would they take ayahuasca? They are not cooped up in buildings cut off from nature.

JEREMY: Their culture is animist.

JAN: That's right, their culture is animist, and therefore they are in a reality model that includes shamanism. It's therapy, medicine. . . . You go see the doctor when you're sick, that's all.

TIGRANE: So what are the basic warnings for anyone already determined to experience this for the first time—since we're not talking of inviting anybody to make this journey?

VINCENT: It's complicated. . . .

JEREMY: The first warning is to say that it is like going off to sea by yourself, and in fact, you do not know how to sail. So, you must be prepared before leaving port alone on your sailboat. In my opinion, it is worth the trouble of spending the most time possible in the library; or, if you do not like to read, speaking with people who have had this experience and learning as much as possible.

JAN: That's a good example, since you are making metaphors.

If you are leaving on a boat for the open sea, you prepare yourself. And you find a good skipper—because you can read all the sailing manuals you want, you will still never learn to be a skipper just from reading a book.

Get prepared: What are you going to run into on a sailboat? It's good to have book knowledge, to know you have to stoop down when the boom passes, to know how to change course, the dangers, to know you need to always wear a life vest, because it is possible to fall into the water at any time. But you are going to find yourself going through periods of loneliness, fear when there are storms, and these are things you cannot prepare for only by reading books.

So, look for practices available in our world, our society, which will help prepare you. For example, Vipassana meditation—I have never done it but it is something that seems interesting to me (maybe I'm kidding myself, in which case I would like your reaction).

All at once, you are going to have different perceptions of the self. Everything that is going to educate us about this is interesting because at a given moment, in the trip, this is going to be the territory . . . this is going to be a discovery. So tension and fear is inevitable.

Try to train yourself to be as if you were on a boat, alone at the prow during a storm. Hike in the mountains by yourself in the rain for two hours; go look for things that are a little intense, on unfamiliar ground.

Work on yourself, on your body. Also ask yourself questions. For example, you are often going to run into the truth of the relationships you have with others. Or, if you're a couple, you are going to have to clearly examine your relationship to see if you have any unfinished business, because things are going to come up and hit you in the face real hard. So, examine this, not necessarily with a therapist, but see where you are at in your life. What were your intentions, your goals; might you have betrayed things you believed in strongly during crucial ages and that left a deep impression? Make a wide circuit like this inside, emotionally.

And then, the final thing—here I concur with Vincent, but I would replace the word *distrust* with *vigilance*. You must be extremely vigilant, where you take it, with whom you take it, how you are going to take it. And to maintain this vigilance, even if everything goes very well, when returning from these altered states, in the way you are going to think about these experiences. I go back to what I said earlier. For me that is the ABC.

VINCENT: I think that working on yourself is extremely important when taking plants like ayahuasca. There is actually a purgative aspect at the beginning, a physical and mental purge. It is a good thing if a person has already begun working on his psychological system and also his body. For example, having fasted, followed a diet, having exercised or played sports as well.

All the toxins we collect during our everyday life are the first things that ayahuasca will attack. So it is not a bad idea to fast or to follow diets based on herbal teas or vegetable soups, or the standard detoxification techniques. It is also a good idea to work on your psychological system, because, initially, it will be all your primary mental layers that will be resonating. If you are already clear with yourself, I think you will be one step ahead in the work that the plant is going to perform.

JAN: Someone told me: "If you haven't dieted—in other words, eliminated from your diet shortly beforehand meat, alcohol, not to mention other toxic substances—if you haven't established some kind of hygiene in your body's physical functioning, you might end up having a super negative trip, you might have the impression of being eaten alive by giant tarantulas, whereas it is perhaps only the ayahuasca finding the remains of some pork chops in your intestines and you are the physical witness of this battle. You can cross through this state, but the more you cleanse, the greater your ability to attain deeper states.

Several people who took ayahuasca for the first time were nailed to the ground, lying down all night with physical pains. And then—boom!—the second or third day, very beautiful visions and a sense of well-being. But first of all, there are corporeal, organic things that need to be cleared before you can see the essential. You have to take out the shovel; this takes place through evacuation. . . . You have to prepare yourself; even if just a little; there is no need to leave for a monastery for three months.

VINCENT: I do not think that spending three months in a monastery is necessarily superfluous. I don't want to be taken for an austere spoilsport. . . .

JEREMY: Are you sure? [Laughs.]

VINCENT: Please excuse me; I am sort of being like the guy who keeps coming back to the same thing, but it seems to me that this is a very important experience and should not be taken lightly. I say this, and at the same time there can be different cases because there are people who can find themselves in an experience like this for entirely circumstantial reasons, and it can be a meeting with their destiny.

It is difficult to prejudge everyone's experience by saying that it must be done this or that way. There is not really any rule. We can deduce the broad lines, but we should not take things literally either. Someone can go to the Amazon while on a Club Med vacation, take a little excursion and take ayahuasca once, and it can turn out to be an extraordinary and very beneficial experience.

What do you think, Jeremy?

JEREMY: I think that for the moment, historically speaking, we have not listened enough to indigenous people, generally and more particularly to shamans. They have long been treated as impostors and charlatans, let's say irrational people. If we listen to what the Indians have exhausted themselves telling anthropologists for more than a century, they are unanimous in saying that shamanism has a dark side. In fact, the shamans say, the nature spirits who are the source of shamanic knowledge are themselves morally ambiguous. Some do evil and some do good. And, the power a shaman uses to heal is the same power used to cause harm. This is recorded in the anthropological literature since as early as Alfred Métraux in the 1940s. Let's try and be epistemologically courteous and assume, for once, that these indigenous people are telling the truth.

We are not as well informed, but they have already been exploring this for a long time and we should have the courtesy of accepting, until proven otherwise, that what they say is true.

So what they are saying is that the shaman is an ambiguous figure. You must always keep your eye on him. Vigilance, vigilance. And this is the role of the community. In fact, one of the problems of neoshamans is that there is not really a community keeping its eye on them—but that's a whole other issue. And so, this guy who knows how to attain what we would call altered states of consciousness comes back with a power—a knowledge that is a power.

Like all power-knowledge, it has a double edge: it can be used in one way or in the other. It amplifies what is inside the human being. And in fact, we have a destructive part and a constructive part. I am simplifying, but inside of every human being there is a predatory killer and there is also a poet and an individual who cherishes life.

The shaman Fernando Payaguajé who wrote the book *Bebedor de yagé* said, and this is something echoed by many shamans, that when you do your apprenticeship, you are in the forest drinking ayahuasca and tobacco juice for months, and the first entities that introduce themselves to you are often negative entities; and you are initially tempted to receive the power-knowledge in order to do harm. Before anything, you must resist this. Therefore, there is a choice.

What's more, let's say you are working with a good shaman; he chose the white side, light, and healing, and for twenty years he has managed to hold the temptation to do harm at a distance. The more he heals people, the more power he gains; the more power he has, the greater his temptation to abuse it. A shaman is never lily white. He is working with power, and power always has two faces. Therefore, there are no clear categories in this world, there is only ambiguity, things that are like and not like, shadow and light, together and interlaced. . . .

Imagine you are a local guy and you have a little power. Yes, you are tempted to dominate others; you are tempted to shoot magic darts at them.

In fact, one of the problems of the shamanic ayahuasca world is the paranoia about sorcery and the magic darts that are flying all over the place. This is not a peaceful world. And it is true that often—the Westerners who turn up in the Pucallpa suburbs have no idea—but there are guerilla zones between shamans, with all the jealousies they have between one another.

Once you have someone whose star is on the rise and has gained a little power, either because he is attracting gringos or he is healing people, the others begin working to pull him down. This is a perfidious and fairly terrible world. Not just anyone can get inside it, casually. So, it is not so surprising that there are all sorts of people who have been disturbed by these kinds of expeditions!

So it is clear that people here do not believe in the ontological reality of sorcery. They say: "All that is just imaginary." But in fact, there are historical examples, clear cases of people who did not believe in the reality of sorcery but who were placed in situations of negative shamanic attacks, who have been shot by darts in fact, and felt bad, depressed, freaked out, seriously unbalanced for months.

Moreover, in certain languages the word for "magic dart," the word for "knowledge," and the word for "power" is the same: it is *yachay* in Quechua.

[Silence.]

And it would seem that the icaros are manifestations of this same thing; the spirits, the knowledge, the power, the darts, and the icaro, all this, are the same. And it is morally ambiguous.

The darts are used to cure, and illnesses are darts. The shaman performing the healing must have the counterpart dart in his belly. You must have the analogous dart inside of you if you wish to extract it from the body of a patient.

JAN: I would say that you must have knowledge about the weapons, including those for defense. A traditional healer, a curandero, has to be able to defend himself. He must be able to work on the negative energy of the individual, and this is with the knowledge—but a higher knowledge—of the negative energy, the dark things with which he comes into contact. He protects himself with things that can be used to attack. A good healer makes use of these things only to protect himself and not to attack. But he has knowledge of them; otherwise he would be unable to protect himself.

JEREMY: He is literally armed with a kind of armor of darts, which protects him from being bombarded by the projectiles of his colleagues.

JAN: Let's imagine the opposite: we human beings are plants. Ayahuasca is a kind of fertilizer that causes you to grow. But it is the very nature of who you are that is going to grow; ayahuasca is going to work upon your personality. If you are someone who has deep, unconscious desires for power, it is going to activate them; if you are someone who is in love, it is going to activate love. But it is only going to activate who you are.

For me, the role of a good curandero is to place guardians over us throughout the length of the ceremony—because the plant that you are is growing at an accelerated pace—to tell us: "Watch out, do not go there, or there, or there. . . ." Afterward, the person will have seen the possibility of going left or right, and he or she will say he or she is cured. No, the real work still remains to be done.

Often we, as Westerners, think that when we come out of the maloca that we are psychologically and physically healed, like when we have been operated on by a surgeon. We think that it is finished. But in fact you are being shown something: the state you are in now for several days, several weeks, is something that you can have. But to have it you are going to have to work at it, every day, in order to see the emergence of what the Indians of India call the *vasanas,* the latent tendencies, because they too are awakened. The heart, empathy, love are going to be awakened, but the heavy things are going to be awakened in the same way. The good healer will try to help you to avoid taking this or that turn.

JEREMY: I am thinking of something practical along the lines of what you are saying. I have noted that, depending upon who you drink ayahuasca with, all at once it opens the hearts of people who are perfect strangers to each other. You find yourself experiencing bursts of generosity that you would not be having in cold, lucid consciousness. So, it is an empathogen as well; and this is not to say that you must be wary of empathy, but let's just say it is worth the effort to keep yourself informed and keep a slight distance in connection to what you can feel during these experiences. I have one rule: during the forty-eight hours after the experience, I take no action in the real world. No matter what I saw in my visions, I do not reach for the telephone right away.

VINCENT: Yes, you have to engineer airlocks so you can decompress, whether they are temporal, geographical, or mental, because the experiences are intense. But fine, listening to you does not necessarily give me any desire to undergo this kind of experience. . . .

JAN: At the same time, we are not masochists.

I've been going back there—it is now seven years—I consider myself an ayahuasquero; this forms part of my practice. I take it regularly; I go two, three times a year to the Amazon, five weeks last year. So, people are going to tell themselves, this guy, if he says all this and goes back there, it is because he is a masochist; what's more, we can see him wriggling around in his films. . . .

No. I think this requires a discipline that is a true knowledge, a vast knowledge. But you should not go there like someone going to India to see a sage: people often confuse the shaman's personality and his knowledge with the profound wisdom of India—great compassion, for example. Shamanism is not a religion; it is a traditional medicine. They are healers, and as you say, there is that knowledge of having to work with heavier, negative powers. This forms part of the Amazonian world.

JEREMY: Just a word about these famous readers who apparently need warning. I am thinking of a group of Swiss teenagers last year on Christmas afternoon. It was a beautiful day, and they went out in T-shirts and sneakers to hike up the mountain where they were caught by a snowstorm that arrived without warning.

They were found early the next morning shivering in a barn that lay at four thousand feet in altitude, and they were rescued. Anybody could have told them beforehand: "Listen to the mountain—don't go there on Christmas Day in sneakers and T-shirts!" But in any event, like my friend Francis Huxley says, the world is "beyond taking advice." You cannot tell people anything; whatever happens people are going to do stupid things. . . .

VINCENT: I agree completely. In this case, one must not say anything.

JEREMY: Wait—

JAN: No, if not, you don't do anything—

JEREMY: Personally, I don't encourage people to do anything other than: love your children, clean up after yourself, simple things like that. I am not trying to encourage anyone at all to do anything, especially taking consciousness-altering substances! But, on the other hand, I feel that everyone has to be free to do what he or she wants, so long as it does not interfere with anyone else. And people can exchange advice. Giving advice is not the same as encouraging people; it is trying to be at the service of a certain knowledge and making it accessible. If people want to inform themselves before going up the mountain on how they should equip themselves, well, let them be able to do so.

VINCENT: Listen, it's not hard for me to share your points of view; I am in basic agreement with everyone in fact. I think that all your points of view are basically correct.

JEREMY: Thanks! [Laughs.]

VINCENT: I would be prone to thinking like you and at the same time . . . at the same time, I do not like talking about the dark side to which you have alluded. I think that these are things that we don't really need to talk about. They also have less power when people do not believe in them. I am not saying they have no power, but if you don't believe in something at all, that something has less chance of getting a grip on you.

JEREMY: You want to leave the shadow in the shadows. . . .

VINCENT: I think that the shadow, either one can cast light on it, or else it is indeed best for it to remain in the shadows. That is my basic opinion on the matter. Now, it is true that these things exist. At the end of the book on iboga, I put in a short chapter on it, explaining to well-meaning Westerners that even if they did not believe in it, if they ever experienced this kind of thing, they would find themselves in a situation where, unfortunately, they would be forced to believe despite themselves.

JEREMY: That's funny; you want to talk about the dangers, and at the same time you don't want to talk about the shadow zones. . . .

VINCENT: I am very ambivalent about this question.

JEREMY: Bravo! [Laughs.]

VINCENT: I think that you have to keep in mind . . . I think that the good is better than the bad, even if there are dimensions where good and evil have no meaning.

JAN: I agree.

VINCENT: . . . This is perhaps a stupid thing to think. We are not necessarily in agreement. It depends upon the situation in which you find yourself.

JAN: What is the good, for oneself? No one wants to do evil. You do not do evil for the sake of evil. You are going to kill your neighbor to have more land so your children can profit from it; it is for the good of your children, your wife, your society, your culture, your race, your religion, your state. . . .

VINCENT: I believe there can be a wide variety of situations here. I am truly open to everything in the sense that I believe that everything can exist; I believe that everything is possible. Actually, the evil of one person is not necessarily the evil for another person.

JEREMY: Yes. That's right.

VINCENT: But to return to what is good and what is evil, I think that it is what was said at the beginning. For example, a shaman can make you experience some extremely difficult things that will appear as negative things to you. . . .

JAN: For your own good.

VINCENT: Everything depends on the purpose of things; everything depends upon the context in which it lies. You say he is tempted by good and evil, excuse me, but why do evil?

I took ayahuasca with some people. Afterward, we were riding the train and the train came to a stop and someone said: "I think that it is thanks to my powers that I have stopped the train." Okay, super! After all, why not? Let's accept this could be true; but what's the point of stopping the train?

JAN: Especially the one you are on! [Laughs.]

VINCENT: Is it too much to ask that people just keep some plain common sense?

JAN: This is what we were talking about at the beginning. We are primitives, babies. Our mind is going to grab hold of the experience, we are going to think that we are prophets—like a child who has power with a television clicker. And the whole task is to deconstruct, to not grab on to things.

VINCENT: But you wouldn't put a pistol in the hands of a child. If an adult sees a child with a gun he is going to tell him: "Put down that big toy before you hurt someone."

JAN: I agree with Jeremy when he says if you want to learn how to hurt people from ayahuasca, it will take fifteen days. The heaviest things, the lowest thoughts that are the easiest to think, the crude desires, all that, is simple. But understanding the mechanisms of these crude desires, understanding them deeply and dying to what one is and to this whole vast world, to go into the jungle for two years, to become a healer, integrating all the power of the negative one has so you can maintain a tense relationship, to not shut your eyes, to not believe that all you are is light . . .

I laugh when I hear people saying: "Ayahuasca is only visions of light." In shamanism, there are negative things and dark powers. Saying that it is only light and that all the healers are sages is being completely out of it when it comes to ayahuasca. I read in Germany: "Come dressed in white with bouquets of flowers." Enough already! So we all agree here, this is not what ayahuasca is.

But I don't understand how people can do negative things with ayahuasca. I can't form the thought in my head; my body tenses up if I try to imagine this possibility. Seeing negative things caused me so much pain that it put my head in the bucket; I clenched my teeth like a reptile when experiencing certain worlds that I was to cross. I am incapable of psychologically imagining how a dedicated shaman could send harm to anyone like this. But I do not think that this is due to my personality but rather to the way, over the course of what is seven years now, I've been trained to perceive this world.

I think that they have methods, as well—

VINCENT: Of course.

JAN: —to avoid a case where the poor tiny Western individuals who can take possession of powerful things quite quickly—like me for example, I might have been subject to that, or like others I have seen. I have seen people, after ayahuasca sessions, trying to turn off the light with the power of their gaze or tricks like that; we are swimming in the basic substance of a primitive sorcery, weak and pathetic. That is what the negative side truly is.

I followed one rule, which was to go with certain kinds of curanderos. I did not want to be given the capability of entering dark things, I did not want the responsibility because I saw that much darkness lived within me and still lives within me. But I attribute this to their way of helping me travel through these worlds.

JEREMY: There is something I thought was important, something Guillermo told me when I interviewed him. It was on the hygiene of power. He said that when you healed someone, when the power traveled through you and you got results, it left you with a kind of intoxication of power. And what was required to get back the good feeling was to go on the diet at this time, go back into your hole, and suffer a little—the spirits really like people who suffer a little, he said—and next empty out this experience so you can go back into action and be able to do good work again.

I can compare this to when I speak in public and there are a couple hundred people in the room. Let's say it all goes well, it gives you a kind of power—

VINCENT: —of intoxication, yes—

JEREMY: —and on the next day, you start over in another town, and you can do this four or five times, on a kind of tour. People might say: "It's brilliant." Journalists ask questions. And a part of me goes stupid because of always saying the same thing. But the ego is puffed up from this experience. So: "Shut up. Go back into your hole; be humble."

VINCENT: I believe this requires constant training. It is a job of always calling yourself into question, of remaining vigilant toward yourself.

JAN: At a certain time, I don't know if this is still valid, the Indians put together communities that consisted of three or four hundred individuals maximum. They had to have a leader but they avoided giving him power over too many people, so they had to find areas of balance. It is interesting because we think they are simply incapable of getting organized; and if we think of our own powerful men, we'll see that history offers few guarantees. You say: "Shamanic power can turn you in to a jerk, so ask for a huge task." I think it is just power plain and simple, whether you are a movie actor or a scientist who has received the Nobel Prize. Once you have earned the recognition of others, or the spirits (perhaps even harder to manage!), that is when you have to be super vigilant.

If someone puts a stick in your spokes, it means you are blazing your own path. It is when society praises you that it is super dangerous. You just have to look at politics. It's frankly obvious that it does not necessarily make people intelligent, wise, sensible.

JEREMY: There is nothing terribly hygienic about an electoral campaign.

JAN: History has not produced very many people like Gandhi or Mandela. They are truly exceptional cases—sages perhaps.

[Silence.]

VINCENT: No one has talked about the benefits, for us, after several years of hindsight. . . .

JEREMY: I find that answering that question is a bit presumptuous, therefore difficult. . . .

Personally, my experience with ayahuasca among the Ashaninca opened me to the reality that I am, quite simply, a part of nature. And that everything my culture has told me about my separation from the rest of nature was an arbitrary, and ultimately false, line contradicted by biological data. We are all made of cells, DNA molecules, and everyone has the same coding system. We are all from the same family, the "double helix" family, which is the symbol of shamanism incidentally.

This forced me to fundamentally rethink how I understand the world, how I understand my own way of thinking: by education I am a humanist rationalist, but self-critical. This has given me another point of view: philosophical, epistemological. And another way to look at the meaning of life. To know that beneath the surface, beyond what my eyes show me, there is a reality that cannot be ordinarily perceived, that teems with intelligence, and that places us on the same plane as birds and flowers.

We form part of this layer of life, and it is a beautiful thing. And this idea that we are the only intelligent beings, the only beings who communicate, is obviously false. If we take the trouble to listen to what is going on in the forest, beneath our feet, among the ants, in our own cells: there are symbolic conversations all day long, and it is cool!

On second thought, one is less alone. Blades of grass are made from cells that send one another the same signals as my own neurons, and therefore grass is just as neuronal and intelligent as me and my brain, and well, it's a beautiful thing!

VINCENT: That's a splendid testimonial. [Laughs.] For me, it has actually radically changed my way of seeing things, for the reasons that you mentioned. It has connected me with a living system much bigger than anything I could ever have imagined as a city dweller. And then, it helped me understand many things.

It connected me with the memory of our species. The experiences I had in Africa truly made me dive deep. Africa is one of the cradles of humanity and this made it a much more profound experience than my experience in the Amazon, because there I was truly able to go back into an archaic state that was almost unfathomable.

And then it really opened my mind, quite simply, to other forms of thought, other forms of being, other ways of being. For me it was a truly overwhelming experience, in the good sense of the word. An overwhelming experience because I was not focused on shamanism, even if I was fairly monomaniacal on the subject for a long time.

Shamanism forced me to become interested in history, geography, science, and to ask myself philosophical and ethical questions on an almost daily basis, even practically from one minute to the next. Why am I doing this? Why am I thinking that? Why am I positioning myself like this? What is the meaning of my actions? How does this fit in, into what history, into what time line? And this allowed me to put all my modern experience into perspective, which is something I found quite interesting.

By connecting with another way of being and with history, especially through this African experience, and then combining all of it, I gained a fuller and richer vision of the individual, in the broad sense.

Now I am no longer having shamanic experiences, in the sense that I am no longer going specially to places where shamanic rituals are held, but this has altered my way of looking at things and seeing the world in a truly constant manner.

JEREMY: And writing, as well?

VINCENT: The writing . . . I went through a period where I needed to give shape to what was happening to me—which concurs with what Jan said earlier—in which the meaning I placed on the experience, the way in which I felt it, were extremely confused and extremely enigmatic for me.

The fact I am able to help myself with artistic expression and writing, which all the same has a very regulating effect on thought, because starting from the moment you are capable of writing, of organizing things with a grammar and language system, and putting them into a novel-like form, with a story that holds together despite all . . . It changed my way of writing for a certain period. Mainly I produced a fairly long novel, one in which I tried to recast this possibility of exploding thought, while not being exploded because a person is still himself. In the end, fine, all of these things. One of the difficulties for Western individuals is this kind of explosion of the ego, return to the ego.

We enter a field of consciousness that is not our ordinary field of consciousness, and we are still obliged, unless we want to become complete yo-yos, to return to reality. Writing helped me do this, and I projected it into my writing. And, having perhaps crossed through the black areas, having seen them in a way that was so present, I have desiderata that are really quite simple: write stories with a happy ending, and send things back to my fellow human beings in a simpler and more positive form. So, I try to write things in a way that makes them more accessible. Quite simply because I have integrated a part of the experience. There you have it.

JAN: It is funny that you talk about making things simpler with a happy ending. At one time, I said much the same thing about cinema.

Cinema is not shamanism, we are quite clear on that. But it offers an experience. The spectator is going to be guided through his emotions, to live, through archetypes that are the actors, by identifying with an image on the screen, and through a story that will force him to encounter things he would not encounter in the everyday world. When we see the transcendent hero on his dragon in the movies whereas we, the only thing we do is cross the street to go to the post office, we experience something.

Lastly, the mythic universe is the thing that makes us vibrate. We are shaped by myth, and through a novel or a film we are offered the possibility to see it come to life in a small way. A story is offered people. And without being moralistic, without separating the good from the bad, I told myself, in comparison to Gaspar Noé's great film *Irreversible,* which is horrible . . . I remember when I was in Peru and leaving the maloca with him, we talked about it, and said: "We suffered tonight; that was terrible." It is like, in the movies, you are scared, you witness murders; but in the morning everything is fine; or else, at the end of your stay, when leaving the shaman, everything is fine. You are happy, you are strong, you have reconnected with your self-esteem, humbly but with strength. You come back out of the maloca in good shape.

Without doing shamanism, there are inevitably things that you communicate; you manufacture not rituals but something that is going to be felt. In a book or a movie, it is the same. So, you can force the spectator to go through anything you like, the most horrible, terrifying things—in any case, this was my point of view—but the question that came up is how someone lets you leave the room. Here it is.

This is truly my main issue. A good shaman leaves me with esteem for myself, the desire to fight, maybe change the system, to react, to change things, to ask questions, or to feel well because I have had a really good laugh. It is not that he is going to change people, but what the filmmaker's intention is with regard to the effect he would like his film to have on the viewers—without thinking that he is making great things, but just the small intention, that is the most important thing. And so, the same thing came to me that came to you: we can force them to go through anything we like but we should not leave them with their heads still in the bucket.

I could not make a film like *Se7en,* even if I adore this film, because you leave people in despair and the world's misery. And Gaspar Noé, whose own world is quite dark all the same, who wants to be provocative, to shake things up, to put people's heads in the bucket, came up with *Irreversible* after spending a week to ten days in Peru. This story ends in tragedy, but as it starts at the end and goes back toward the beginning, this story ends by love, so it still leaves a feeling of love at the end.

This is an interesting phenomenon. I really had it in for him during the magisterially terrifying rape scene, and at the end, I told myself: "Hold on, I think that his passage through ayahuasca changed him, ultimately." So here I am speaking bluntly about someone else; perhaps he will deny it, Gaspar, who might say: "No, that's an idiotic thing to think." In any case, this altered my relationship to my personal creation, being a filmmaker and making movies, in this way: concentrating my efforts on how to end.

If not, what has been changed? I concur with what both of you say. To say it in another way, yesterday I was with my children in La Villette to see an exhibit on extraterrestrials, who come from other remote worlds. . . . And at the end, we saw a scientist who said: "We do not know if there is life in the universe, but it seems possible that there is, and we are developing instruments in our telescopes that have been so perfected that perhaps in this generation"—and I could see my kids' eyes bugging out listening to this person—"perhaps we will finally witness humanity's meeting with another intelligent race in the universe."

And I said to myself: "That's wonderful; this is what they, the Indians, gave me. They helped me meet the extraterrestrials that people are looking for in the depths of the universe but that are in fact in the garden next door, with whom we can communicate, who bring us things, and actually change our perception of our life and knowledge." I said to myself: "It is the alchemist who travels all around the world to look for something that was right next to him all the time, it is the eternal myth, and our civilization has been carried away by this eternal myth of hunting in the deepest depths of the universe for something that lies within." The shamans have seen this, and because they have passed it along to us have changed our perception of reality, and our relationship to the planet and to the other species.

A plant, if we watch its growth speeded up on film, it has a life, it has an intelligence, it knows how to position itself. It was there long before us. It is our grandparents, it is our ancestors, and we are not even capable of weaving a connection with something that is right at our own front door; and the Indians invited me inside. I trembled and wept, and it completely enriched my vision of life, reality.

I return to Peru regularly. I have gone looking in other areas. I have gone looking in India, Tibet. I made films on the sages, but my deepest ties are with traditional Shipibo-Conibo medicine. I take ayahuasca with other Shipibo shamans along the upper Ucayali; I am staying with the same traditions. Perhaps this will end someday; I have only been doing this for seven or eight years.

I have gone through phases of complete imbalance with regard to my society, with regard to myself, with regard to my emotions. And then little by little, over time, I have come to agree with you: it is acquiring the ability to integrate these kinds of experiences, to not just barge in.

I went for fifteen days, taking ayahuasca every evening. I no longer knew if it was day or night, I kept going because I had access to this secret book no one had ever shown me; and this book told me essential things that no one in the whole library had ever told me before.

JEREMY: You're an extremist. . . .

JAN: I am an extremist, definitely. You close this book and your sole desire is to start reading it again because it brings you things. But you have to take the plane to go live in the jungle, so you are not feeling too good. And then, little by little, because this is a book about balance, a time will come when it tells you: "One of the first things to do is form a balanced relationship with the book itself."

This is one of the keys to balance in the relationship with the plant: knowing how to integrate. You will not be able to go there for a year, and that is fine. Because you should feel fine everywhere, you should be fine at home, in life, in the very depths of the subway.

If the plant brings you anything, if shamanism brings you anything, it is how to have good relations with others, with people, and if you are not happy and you realize that things are not working, it is because there is a problem. Generally, you have to stop, or else you end up completely confused. Therefore: pay attention that the signals you're getting are good and your thoughts are on the positive side, that you are cooler and not as stressed, and that your desire to find this book in the library is shrinking, et cetera.

You work and you make things; you find a balance between your personal life, your profession, and your trips to visit the Indians. Fine, I've invested time in this; I have gone through difficult phases, but I have the impression of having grasped this: to listen to what the shamans and the plant are giving you, because it comes from this combination.

You mentioned simplicity. You know, when I made the film about Amma, she said some things that were super simple, and I recall that there were some individuals who poked fun at her because in order to be a great Indian sage, you have to say great metaphysical things and grand conceptual phrases. But I thought what she did, giving only short aphorisms, was brilliant. Like: "Why are people worried about owning the biggest vacuum cleaners, ones that suck up the smallest particle of dust, when they are not capable of cleaning the filth in their minds," and so on.

Little things, because in the same way we are removed from the intelligence in nature by seeking it in the depths of the cosmos, it is good to start first by cleaning the simple things on our floors; to have a simpler thinking process, devoted to the things of life, this world, and not go off in a tailspin of concepts every moment by leaving the present moment.

To conclude, I discovered that I had many metaphysical questions. I come back to *Dune* and what I said when we began. What is God? Death? I believe this is part of human programming to a certain extent, but it helped cleanse me. I no longer ask questions about God; this is not because I've met God, not at all, but that my thoughts no longer go there. The great metaphysical questions are ones you don't ask, I don't know why. It forms a part of being happy, of feeling things.

JEREMY: There is one element that I am particularly fond of: gorillas refuse to take the intelligence tests that scientists try to give them. Every time someone has created a test to evaluate gorillas, they have extremely low scores, but it is because they are too intelligent to take them seriously!

When you stand in front of a gorilla, you are in front of a creature that weighs five times more than you, it has a head as large as yours, and has pensive eyes. . . . This is clearly not a stupid animal, it is in your best interests to treat it politely, and finally I love this idea that nobody has any clue to what is going on in a gorilla's head because we are not yet smart enough to step past our own anthropocentricism.

JAN: Shipibo means "man-ape." . . .

JEREMY: Hold on, in Amaringo's paintings you can see man-apes smoking pipes while lying in hammocks that are anacondas. . . .
[Break while the participants go out for a meal.]

IBOGA

VINCENT: Iboga brings up another problem. It is a psychotropic substance that has recently appeared on the scene like ayahuasca—it has only been a short while since their existence has become public knowledge.

I went to Gabon, in Africa, to follow the initiation of a tradition called Bwiti. It is an extraordinary experience, but one that is quite tough. While stressing the warning side, it has to be pointed out to our contemporaries that the prohibition of these psychotropic substances is depriving them of an impressive learning tool. What's more, this prohibition arises from our lack of an "adult" attitude toward these substances.

Iboga—and this is one of the specific features distinguishing it from ayahuasca—forces you to go back into your memory, your own memory but also really into the memory of the species. So, you can really connect to a system of knowledge that is incredibly interesting, and that is very mentally accessible. Iboga inspires thinking, which is not like ayahuasca where you go off on a colorful trip. With iboga, everything is highly structured, and this also implicates the mind. That is what is not so easy to integrate, psychically.

MICHKA: So, if you had to sum up, why you suffered so much?

VINCENT: On the one hand, I think there were not many Westerners who had done this stuff at the time I did. Next, I did it in conditions that were completely "local," with Gabon natives who were initiated with us, and even for them, it was really tough.

So, here you are being initiated with iboga, which is a super strong drug, you have one hundred fifty blacks dancing around you, you are in the middle of the jungle; basically it's a world away from everything you are used to; on the other hand it can quickly bring to mind those bad B movies you watched as a teenager.

But fine, whatever doesn't kill you makes you stronger, and after going through a kind of hazing—I have to say that I stuck to it; I returned to Gabon four times until I got over a hurdle—eventually things became clear.

This is the reason, given the difficulties I had, that while I can say to guys like you: "It is an extraordinary experience, try to do it if you get the chance," I think it would be wrong for me to tell the fans of Tintin and Spirou: "Hey guys, you should all head down to Gabon and get scarified." [Laughs.]

JAN: I just had Anne on the phone and she told me something.

There is a French healer, a very strong eighty-five-year-old woman. She gave me an auscultation once and told me: "You have energy leaks— an appendicitis scar from when you were fourteen." She pinched my skin and did manipulations on me. Afterward I was unable to sleep for several days because of all the energy I had.

Because she is getting old, she has been training someone who is an osteopath to continue her specific technique. Anyway, Anne went to see her, and the grandmother said to her: "I am going to tell you a story. I have been training somebody for years, and the other day his wife came to tell me he was dying. I went back into his room, and there were actually different energy bodies scattered about the room; it was a complete jumble. He said he was seeing dead people and was dying."

The old woman put the fellow back together, and everything was restored to order; and, in fact, he had taken iboga the day before.

VINCENT: No kidding?

JAN: He pulled himself out of it, he was able to get back; but when all's said and done, this is something that is too hot to handle. . . . Warning: ayahuasca or iboga, do not take them when you are alone.

VINCENT: Right! The problem with this kind of experience is that the B film scenario is sometimes really on the menu.

[Silence.]

JEREMY: So, how are we going to do this? We could start with: how to be during the visions.

JAN: We will start with that, and after we will look at its therapeutic effectiveness.

VINCENT: For visions . . . Like you said, you must do whatever you can, try to keep a stiff upper lip, be as courageous as you possibly can when experiencing something really strong. There are some things you can master and some things you can't. On the other hand, it is very important that the shaman always leave you on a positive note when it is over, and you should try to understand why whatever you could not master remained beyond your grasp so you can do better next time.

JEREMY: Keep a stiff upper lip but breathe; and breathe.

VINCENT: Whatever the truly black or difficult sequences you go through may be like, try to work back through them to a new place. Normally the shaman will bring you there with his songs; he is there to accompany you. I also think it is up to each person to gradually find the right tools so they can do it themselves.

JEREMY: This is some good advice I received from an Ashaninca shaman: when you are drowning in visions, look for the shaman's melody and hook your mind to that melody. Listen to it. It is like a rope: you can use it to get out when you are submerged by a vision, when you are dying, when you cannot breathe. Or else, quite frankly, pray—and I am saying this as an agnostic. It seems to me that if there is ever a time for praying, even as an agnostic, then this is the time. Or else, you can also smoke tobacco.

JAN: At the beginning when you enter and sit down to begin the session, do not expect anything in particular. You will have models, like the relaxation model we talked about earlier, complete physical relaxation with a kind of peace and tranquillity that gently keeps your thoughts solely in the room with the others. Do not try and have visions when in this relaxed state. Simply center yourself in your belly, your guts, and feel; relax as much as possible; and keep doing this when you start feeling the effects of the ayahuasca. Do not try to resist the effects; simply stay concentrated on the relaxed state of your body.

What Jeremy said is absolutely correct: cling to the songs, try to fix your mind on the shaman's songs because they are not only the rope that will pull you from the water but also the one that will let you go up in space. And avoid being in a state of expectation because otherwise you will attract the mind, you are going to lie in wait for reactions.

Try to tell yourself that you are listening to gentle chants, that you are at peace with everyone else there, that it is not possible to die a priori by taking ayahuasca (the lethal dose is six quarts!). This is important, because an instantaneous feeling of imminent death can arise, but this is simply virtual, a thought that is going to germinate in the mind: "Oh, I am dying." It is the thought that is dying for a moment, not you.

You must breathe in rhythm with the shaman's breaths for this thought to dissolve, for your organs to relax, because it is simply the discovery of new things. If people are making noise because they are vomiting or crying, concentrate on your own experience, don't start: "Damn, that guy giggling on the left or the person weeping on the right are bothering me." Because that is how you are going to cut yourself off from your own experience. Try both to be with the shaman and to not entertain negative thoughts about the people around you, just because they are irritating you. You should humbly tell yourself at the start: "I am here for nothing except to listen, to meet the plant, to feel good, and try to get through this thing." Afterward, visions or no visions will arrive, but it is a good door to use to enter.

Next, if the visions are strong, or the intoxication is intense, your first impulse will be to try to get up and leave, to go into the light, to get out of there although this is a moment of understanding. It is just because it is new, so, even if it is beautiful, if it is too strong, you'll be scared.

If dark visions are attacking you, you should not reject them as something from outside that is attacking you personally. Just tell yourself that you are in contact with a suffering, negative, or maybe even a slightly heavy physical part of yourself, that maybe the image is heavy because all at once your mind finds itself in contact with your guts. . . .

Do not reject the dark things but instead try to relax and allow them to pass through you. Don't try to push them away for they will always come back. It's like fear: if you try to think of something else to avoid being scared, you enter into a vortex of fear; on the other hand, if you try to relax . . . The body is your refuge; this is something I truly believe. If your body is feeling good, there will be less space in your head for fear.

If the trip is too strong, if you think you are leaving your body, try to touch it, relax it, put your hand on your stomach, curl up in a ball, and let it do what it wants.

Try to get through this and then don't start telling yourself too many stories the next morning. You said: take notes. Why not? But don't tell yourself too many things, be wary of thoughts about yourself of this nature: "I am someone like this, et cetera." In other words, the immediate attempt to cling to the experience. Try to stay calm, like you said, before taking action in the world. Hold on to the feeling and do not try to interpret it, at least not right away.

Let several hours go by, that's always good. And it's the same when talking about your visions: it is good to hold back a small territory for yourself to hold certain things and not necessarily express them at once. Try to let things gently find their proper place inside.

JEREMY: Even if you are a diehard materialistic atheist, it is the kind of experience that, it's true, puts you in contact with things touching on death, on life before and after death, and that touch on souls, both incarnated and disincarnated.

So it is clear that here we are in the middle of a territory where there are people who don't believe in the reality of these kinds of things, and we have to admit that no one knows with any certainty just what a soul is, or a spirit. So, we are in a territory that is ontologically indeterminate. Nonetheless, ayahuasca, and iboga, too, it seems to me, precipitate you, even if you are a materialist, rationalist, atheist academic, into a sphere that is the spitting image of the one described by shamans the world over, filled with disincarnate entities, dead people, people who are not yet born, talking animals, and all sorts of things.

So you cannot enter it with impunity; it is not like going to the movies. And when you are there, in the experience, you are in the midst of contemplating your own death.

I have a science journalist friend who is pretty much a Darwinian, who came with me to have an ayahuasca experience. At the end of the session, he had one question for the shaman: "Why, when you go into the world of ayahuasca, is there such a feeling of the proximity of death?"

VINCENT: That's amusing, I never felt that. . . .

JEREMY: And the Ashaninca shaman replied that ayahuasca is like that. It causes you to leave the world of the living and brings you to the other side. It brings you close to death, and next it brings you back to life; and this gives you more life, in fact, the fact of leaving this world and going into the world of the dead and souls. It is somewhat mortifying, it petrifies you, but then you come back.

"I have the impression of dying but I am not dying" is almost a mantra. "It is going to be okay. I have taken a hallucinogenic drug; I think I am dying but I am not really dying. Oh yes, and my heart is my friend." It all comes back to the body, as you said.

These experiences caused me to appreciate my body more. They gave me the desire to be healthy, to feed it a healthy diet, to take it for walks every day, like a dog, you know: "An hour in the forest, let's go!"

When you return to life, it is "Long live life! Long live this planet!" And you realize that your life is a gift, your body is a gift. . . . It is a beautiful thing.

VINCENT: We can say a few words about coming down, too. . . . It is true that very simple remedies like taking a good cold shower, going out for a run, a good breakfast . . . When you have undergone three days of intense experiences, it is the little things that can be most effective.

JEREMY: Cold shower, going out for a run, ayahuasca . . . [Laughs.]

VINCENT: It is true that it is important to reconnect afterward; this is where you reintegrate the experience. And athletic activity so that your body integrates the experience, so it does not remain something superficial that dissolves soon afterward, is worth the effort.

TIGRANE: Should a time be set aside in advance for reintegration with no need to rush things?

VINCENT: That depends a little on your material possibilities. When you have the experience in a foreign country, you still have the plane ride back home for decompressing. It is true that the shock can be quite rough, for different reasons. The conceptual systems are not the same; and an experience like this will open perceptions that are customarily not opened when you are moving about a large city. And in a large city like Paris, what could be labeled with a somewhat reductive and generic New Age term as the "energies" are not necessarily that great. There is an enormous amount of stress; you can be assaulted by noise; in the streets, people are not necessarily smiling.

JEREMY: Why is "energy" a New Age concept? Unless, this is what you are calling people's attitudes?

VINCENT: In any case, it is obvious for the people who have taken something like this that this kind of experience is going to increase your sensitivity, so you are definitely going to capture larger bands of frequency than usual. It is obvious that what the city of today reflects back is something quite hard and aggressive, if only trying to get through traffic jams, just after you have gotten back from Peru. . . .

There are techniques for this, too: we all have energy centers that we can more or less master, and we must get our bodies, and our energetic bodies, used to opening and closing through an act of will. The ability to move from one state to another is something we should harness. People should manage to figure out how to do this because otherwise they can remain in a state of hypersensitivity. This shows up by being easily irritated, having anxieties, things like that.

JAN: For example, the fact that you may have experienced total ecstasy and two days later you are completely depressed.

JEREMY: What's more, you can use all the ruses and techniques you want. . . . You can take a week to decompress on site, take baths, and all that, and after your plane lands you envision a cool week, you go see a masseur, its wonderful. . . . But, in the final analysis, these are two different worlds, there is nothing you can do about that. It is hot and cold; and the forest versus the metal machine. We are in a culture. . . . This is a caricature, but it is technological and a little hard-edged; it also makes things difficult with its constant bombardment of the senses with information through an array of screens—you get the picture.

So, even with all the massages in the world, how can you be bicognitive without becoming schizophrenic? Well, dear friends, this comes about by going through a schizophrenic phase. [Laughs.]

VINCENT: It is exactly like that.

JEREMY: And afterward you become bilingual by dint of being schizophrenic.

JAN: It is a question of training. I love coming back to the city after the jungle, now.

JEREMY: Now that you know how!

JAN: Now that I am used to it, it is no longer depressing. There are other advantages: you have more comforts.

JEREMY: I have noticed that jaguar energy is not very productive at the supermarket. Intelligent, that can be all right, but the thing: "I am a wild animal, I am a predator, I am a bit savage," there are specific places in our world where this doesn't work well, and the supermarket is one of them. Test it yourself.

JAN: It's true there are times . . . the mosquitoes, the heat, the ayahuasca, the hard life in the villages, all that; I am happy to get there, to go through it, but during the final days, it still feels liberating when I have come home after taking ayahuasca every day for fifteen days. When I leave, the last day, it's like . . . whoosh! I got through it, whew.

JEREMY: Let's be perfectly clear, it is an ordeal.

VINCENT: It is an ordeal, and it is very important to say so. There might be those who take ayahuasca at the Club Méditerranée, but when you go take it in a more roots situation, then you actually get the whole package: sleeping on the ground, not able to wash like you are used to, the mosquitoes, the heat. . . .

JAN: The experience!

VINCENT: The experience, which is hard . . . and all of this truly constitutes an ordeal.

JAN: Over time it has gradually gotten less hard, but until fairly recently every time I went into the maloca, it was an ordeal. You have to go there though. If someone suggests you go to the restaurant next door . . . You must not listen to that little voice telling you: "You are a little too tired, you may be too scared tonight. . . ."

Once the session begins, after a very short time, once the shaman has taken charge and profound contact has been established, all this goes away because the experience dominates, and dawn finds you very content and happy. You say to yourself: "What an imbecile I was to still be so apprehensive last evening." And the apprehension is going to come back the next night. Now, things are all right, I am more laid back, but I think that I've rarely gone there without these apprehensions. Except right at the beginning!

VINCENT: The beginning is the obstetrician of awareness. . . .

JEREMY: You see, we three are living proof that you can enter this perfectly stupid and ignorant, straight from the suburbs of the Western world. It hits you right in the face and this is what specifically stimulates you to move your butt.

JAN: I don't know if you've had this, but I've had difficult phases, when I was discouraged, but I went back anyway because things were not going any better here. Once I took the plane telling myself I was taking the plane to go die over there, that it was my destiny.

These are mental fabrications, paranoid feelings that you grab onto, fears you stumble into, but I think it's crazy when I think back years later how I caught the plane once telling myself that I was going to die in the jungle, and had it all mapped out.

And once I was there, I experienced a symbolic death. It is interesting: psychologically I knew something was going to happen. I was just mistaken about the reality of the experience.

But during the time I was there, it was tough. I was scared day and night, but I had to go on. There was a force inside me that made me continue. I often say: "I've had a history where this was like a stroke of lightning that carried me away completely," but perhaps there are other means, a more level-headed method.

I did one session after another every day for a while, because I was not doing anything else. When I go for five or six days, I go to the maloca every evening because I am only there for a five-to-six-day period, but if I go there for two weeks, I know that I will take breaks, or I simply meditate. When I feel that a session has been strong, I cannot drink the brew, and just listen to the songs.

JEREMY: There is a tendency among Westerners, and some Amazon shamans have noted it, to get fixed on performance when taking hallucinogens. "I should take them; I have to profit from my trip. I have to take them every two nights. I am here for three weeks, I must take it at least seven times minimum, or even every evening"—these kinds of considerations.

Several shamans have asked me: "But why are the people from your culture like this?" And it is a good question.

I believe that no matter what, we remain centered on results and on getting a return out of our investment. While in fact, let's say you have planned for five sessions, and at the end of two or three—

VINCENT: You lose your footing—

JEREMY: You stop because it is too much, instead of telling yourself: "Oh no, I've got to get my money's worth, I am going to do the five all the same and it will give me a kick in the pants." No, I find it worth it to listen to that little voice that is telling you: "Two, that is already quite a lot. . . ."

VINCENT: It's always the same; you have to weigh the pros and cons. Don't give in to your natural inclination for idleness or, as Jan said, the voice will propel you to go eat in a restaurant instead of drinking ayahuasca. And to also know not to pull too hard on the rope at a certain time, because it will let you better integrate the experience . . . instead of letting yourself go under. It is really up to everyone to find the arrangement that works best for him.

JEREMY: There is something we touched on earlier that I would like to go back to, in the area of the ABCs of advice during visions.

I find that one thing that keeps turning up is that, at the beginning, you realize all your weaknesses: "What an imbecile I am!" And then you are in a somewhat indigenous world as a white man, and you realize all the stupidity of your own culture, as well as of yourself.

Next, you see in this wave you are receiving or in this emotional force of sorrow, there is a kind of self-importance that is bluntly symptomatic of what you are seeing; you are not even important enough to deserve the feeling of being ashamed.

So, obviously you are mortal, you are not perfect. "I am imperfect, I am half baked and it is hitting me square in the face: this is doing me some good, please send more my way." In any event, accept this fact. After you have had a certain number of these experiences, you know it is profoundly true, not only while you are having visions, but in general. This will help you take yourself less seriously.

The next time you show up at a session, the less seriously you take yourself, the less ayahuasca will punish you for being self-important. So, it is also an apprenticeship. And your feeling of being scared but still being attracted is because you know you run the risk of getting your ass kicked every time you take ayahuasca. You are going to be confronted with your own stupidity; you are going to be shown the film of all your most recent sins. For one or two hours you are going to be in this uncomfortable place where you are going to have to watch this movie, before you are able to go further.

It is almost like going to the dentist. I don't want to go but I know that it is good for me to go once a year. If you pay good attention to your dental hygiene for the eleven preceding months and go there with a Zen attitude, well, in the end, it will go a lot better than anticipated.

How to experience a good session? To have your first ayahuasca lesson, and enjoy an experience without any jolts and that is problem free, is very rare. It is good for you to have some jolts and problems to contend with for a time: chalk it up to experience. And after a moment, if you are a good learner, you devote your life to it, you take yourself less seriously, you live your life more hygienically, and you have less to fear from these sessions.

[Silence.]

JAN: When you tell people: "In any case, tell yourself that what you are going to meet is you," this provides an additional fear factor, because we know when someone has an imbalance between what he is and what he thinks he is, whether there are discords, or arrangements, or buried fears. What's more a lot of times people will reply: "Actually, I don't really have any great desire to do this."

JEREMY: It should simply be said that this is not everyone's cup of tea.

VINCENT: We should make it clear though that these are extreme experiences and will not appeal to everybody. If I tell someone a detail from what has happened to me, I think the person is going to faint: "But you are a complete nut!"

Everyone has his own desires and peculiarities, and what's more, when it comes to learning, I think that there are tons of different ways and that we do not have to focus primarily on psychotropic substances. You are a little more "aware." But there are other initiatory ways that are all just as effective.

JEREMY: All just as effective?

VINCENT: It seems that way to me. What do you think?

JEREMY: Which ones?

VINCENT: But nothing other than the world one is in, science, I don't know. . . . All the Western concepts have helped me understand the experiences I've undergone, quantum physics, astrophysics, all these things that were utterly foreign to me before. Scientists are highly evolved people, even if they are not necessarily very open and perceptive; they do have access to extremely precise information.

JEREMY: I agree with you there.

VINCENT: There are initiatory systems and meditation systems that are quite interesting. Ayahuasca will resonate with some people and not necessarily with others.

JAN: We are talking about a technique about which we know only a little; that's the reason we're talking together. I think that some of these states can be attained through meditation, but it takes years of assiduous practice.

But for a person like me—a little like something out of a Tex Avery cartoon—who fidgets a lot and needs some heavy raps from a club to calm down—

JEREMY: The nutty squirrel—

JAN: —who needs a heavy rap from a club to be stopped cold. So when you get clubbed in the head, you get clubbed in the head, but if it's well done . . . [Laughs.]

I think the equivalent would be the Tibetan practice of Dzogchen, with forty-nine days in complete darkness. But it's hard to spend forty-nine days in the dark! Or, I don't know, stay in a sensory deprivation tank for a week. . . .

You have to have a little rock and roll in you, I would say. There's, like we said before the side that's a little New Age, in white and all that; and it's funny, when I go to Peru with people, the Indians really like my buddies who don't always shave, have one foot crossed over the other, and who seem more like rockers.

Knocking on muted matter, if you have been a little ahead, is interesting. I am not necessarily talking about those who listen to heavy metal, but look at Alex Gray. He began by dissecting bodies, observing organic matter, then diving right in. Or when you shoot a gore film, not to be scared at the sight of blood but open up the little animal that you are and look inside. This is a warrior's action; it reveals a personality ready to confront its own nature and its material components, one that is not shocked by this or rather what it is not: angels, elves, and cut off from a part of itself.

All the same, we are heaps of impulses that sometimes organize into thoughts, emotions, feelings; but there is this wild aspect you run in to, so you can be scared like a little bird. If you have some rock 'n roll inside, this part does not immediately scare you. Afterward, those who will be the most rock 'n roll are not necessarily those wearing leather.

Rock 'n roll could describe the old Shipibo women healers. The woman I saw, for example, Olivia Arevalo, had me talking to myself: the ability to be this woman, to be able to transcend life, death, fear . . . The next day, I could not get within thirty feet of her. I asked myself: Who is this woman? Conan the Barbarian, next to her, is a little shit.

JEREMY: I find that there is a rock'n roll aspect to this ayahuasca shamanism. What characterizes a shamanic ayahuasca performance are cheap effects and a musical performance centered on a charismatic singer who induces a trance. And the difference is that shamans heal while rock and rollers don't necessarily.

VINCENT: So wouldn't this be the right moment to talk about the quid of the healing? Is shamanism effective?

JEREMY: We should note that good rockers can. . . . In any case, everyone walks away after a concert with a huge smile plastered on their faces. You have been in a trance, a kind of ecstasy. You have been taken into the stratosphere and sent soaring. When you leave a concert your feet hardly touch the ground.

JAN: Definitely. A really good DJ can bring you . . .

JEREMY: It feels good.
[Silence.]

VINCENT: So, the quid of the healing, Jeremy.

JEREMY: The first thing to say is that shamanism is the oldest healing tradition on the planet. We should rather be talking about shamanisms in the plural, the different techniques, but these approaches that use trance and modification of consciousness are the oldest tradition. And yet, its therapeutic effectiveness has not even been studied by science. It is really a shame!

Like it is really a shame that until now no sheriff of rationalism has showed up in places where shamanic practice is still alive, like the Peruvian Amazon, for example. There is no excuse for not going there: they are there and they are still practicing.

Let's take a thousand patients with known, diagnosed conditions, both by doctors and shamans, and judge the therapeutic effectiveness in precise terms. How is it possible that science has failed to assess the therapeutic effectiveness of the world's oldest healing tradition?

Well, it is because of a little thing called epistemological racism; we are talking five hundred years of colonialism here. Why didn't the victors take the medical knowledge of those they defeated seriously? The answer is in the question. So more research is urgently needed, one could say. There you have it. I would love to see a serious and scientifically measured consideration of the therapeutic effectiveness of shamanism. Period.

VINCENT: And, Jan, what do you think?

JAN: I can only agree. . . . I can offer my feelings from having crossed paths with people having problems who went to see the shamans, which is logical, as we are talking about medicine, indigenous medicine.

In any case, I have noticed that there are high success rates—and I am only talking about Shipibo ayahuasca shamanism—for psychological illnesses. They are very, very good at treating depression, for the reason mentioned earlier.

You said: "You take a trip to the spirit world, when you come back you are happy to be alive, you have recovered your self-esteem, you have expanded your perspective, in balance between the seventh floor and the subway, which is the psychological plane in which you have been living. In a mere moment you have expanded this plane to include the sky, nature spirits, stars, and the earth." This aspect exists; it is simply recalling certain things about the magic of life. So I have found them to be pretty effective on depressed people, on psychological problems. Beyond that . . .

VINCENT: But is this something you have observed?

JAN: I can provide examples.

VINCENT: Cite ten or fifteen people who were a little depressed, who went through sessions, and who . . . ?

JAN: Okay, I will cite them for you. For example, one woman who was a doctor and who was around forty years old. One evening—she had been taking ayahuasca for several days—since the start of the session she had been crying, she was really hurting. A session that starts this way is very hard. You are inside your own thing and all of a sudden you hear someone in pain, someone who is moaning in the dark. She cried, wept, this was really quite hard. The shaman focused his attention on her, but only briefly.

In the morning everyone told their experiences. She told me that she had discovered things connected to her childhood; that she had reexperienced times when she had been fondled as a little girl; she saw how it had altered her relations with men throughout her whole life. This was why she was crying. And at the end of the ceremony, she was collapsed in a heap, and she forgave the person who had done this to her, because it was a kind of chain, and she had broken it.

I saw her several years later, and I had the impression that she had gone through a very difficult experience but one that had changed her, changed her relationships, and simply the way she looked at the world.

I have been shocked during my different journeys, when crossing paths with people, women, and seeing this was something that was really quite widespread. I had often thought there was some abuse on young girls, on children in our culture. But it was not something I had any personal experience of and I thought it existed, I don't know . . . somewhere along the lines of one in a thousand, and were serious social mishaps. In fact, through ayahuasca, I realized that it happened much more frequently.

And I could cite several more examples of this kind, accompanied by sometimes amazing transfigurations. For example, there was one young woman, who was around twenty, who started weeping and crying. It was almost like something out of *The Exorcist,* something truly terrifying to see, her eyes rolled up. . . . And in the morning she talked, while crying, about things of this nature.

When I saw her again two years later, she told me about the poetry she had written, and the songs, with a luminous smile I had never seen before, because all I had seen was her pain. A posteriori, by the way, this touched me a great deal; I said to myself: "What a terrible chain she was bearing."

You see, I have given you two examples in the same sense, where very strong positive transformations truly took place.

Afterward, I saw things that were less intense, people who were simply a little calmer, a little more at peace, happier. I have a third category of people, those who are changed after the experience, are more calm and serene, and who, six months later, have made no effort and become restless and hyper like squirrels. Sometimes, I've been a member of this group.

I have also seen more or less well-balanced individuals, who lived fairly uneventful lives, who all at once became fascinated by this and decided to enter into the cycle of initiations, and there I've witnessed accidents.

There are two categories: those who simply come to rebalance, to encounter ayahuasca, to follow a cure; and then those who come see the healers and say: "I want to learn." It is among those who want to learn where I've seen disasters. When he goes back to ordinary life, the person decides to be a kind of shaman and tells himself he is going to organize healings, that he can help people who are truly ill, whereas . . .

Shamans are a little like brain surgeons; and because you spend a little time with them, you can become a kind of nurse, meaning you can give aspirin or make a poultice once the shaman has cleansed the wound. Once you have returned to your tribe, you can give aspirin. And the person gets into a thing—I have seen this several times—which is to sever the bond that has been woven, to say to himself: "I am continuing by myself," to enter mental states that are too strongly tied to the invisible world.

I've gotten phone calls from people who said: "I have shamanic attacks; I am fighting every night." I said: "Be a good fellow; stop taking this and calm down." "But no, you don't understand. . . ."

I say this in the documentary; I myself am an example. At one time I told myself: "Good, I'm going to continue by myself." I continued and got into some real problems. And I had to go back to the Amazon to get myself put back together to some degree.

When you begin a practice with ayahuasca, listen to the healer; it is extremely important. If he tells you: "Don't eat this food," you must not tell yourself you are above that. If he tells you: "You can take this plant for working," you can take it but not if you do not feel you are ready.

I have seen people who remained stuck, who had a very, very strong spiritual experience and then told themselves: "I am the reincarnation of the Virgin Mary," and I respond: "Listen, this is what happened to me, I went to Peru and I thought that. . . ." But you can easily see in their eyes what they are really thinking: "Yes, for you it was just something you thought, but it is true for me."

It is terrible because there is no longer any place to hold on to, so there is only time. Time that ensures the person comes back down, will tell himself that he is cutting himself off from others, to realize he's only kidding himself.

I've often seen people land on their feet. Even, after a little time and going through thresholds of decompression, these people are finally much more solidly anchored in life. I was scared for two or three of them, but up to now the stories have all had a happy ending.

VINCENT: I think we should explicitly say and in no uncertain manner that this can do no good for people who already have large psychological problems.

JEREMY: That's clear.

VINCENT: Actually, I think it can help someone with a substantial psychological hang-up, something that might take five years of psychoanalysis to unravel and take apart while one session of ayahuasca or another psychotropic substance with a good shaman could really explode and untie this knot. But someone who already has serious structural disorders of the psychotic schizophrenic kind, I categorically believe that they could become even worse after, therefore—

JEREMY: No hallucinogens.

VINCENT: Schizophrenia affects seven hundred thousand people. That means 1 percent of the population of France is on antipsychotics for the long term.

JAN: I don't know, I have mixed opinions about schizophrenia. I compare taking ayahuasca to a transcendental schizophrenic stage: schizophrenia for me, a priori, is a state of knowledge.

The person can be divorced from reality, but this individual has no guide and so becomes a danger to herself and to others. But a schizophrenic can be initiated. Just what is schizophrenia? It is when the different parts of your personality are no longer connected. William Blake said: "If a Fool would persevere in his Folly, he would become wise."

When you take ayahuasca—I am talking from my own experience—you realize that you can experience joy and sorrow almost simultaneously. Vertigo suddenly sets in and you're asking yourself: "Who am I? This sorrow or that joy?"

My personality, my identity fractures. Out of this fracture, identity dies and is then reborn. Guided by the shaman, all of this goes well; it is a process. At one moment, I heard voices on both sides of my head, one shrieking in fear and the other with joy. I was caught in a kind of schizophrenic crisis, scientifically guided by the shaman. It was pure science fiction. In short, after coming out of that, I told myself: "Hold on, the schizophrenics . . ."

I later learned that some guys had made an encephalogram of a Shuar shaman who had taken ayahuasca. He was a healer; he sang and they recorded it. They looked at the encephalogram. There was nothing distinctive about it. They even compared it to different encephalograms and they found that it was quite close to the encephalogram of a schizophrenic in full crisis—except the shaman was not a schizophrenic in full crisis. He was aware and working with the plant in the spirit world. Next, there is another bit of information that is interesting: the Indians believe that the madman goes into the world of the spirits like the shaman, except he does not come back; he remains possessed by the spirits.

VINCENT: There is still a sizeable difference all the same.

JAN: It is enormous. I remember going to Saint Anne's Hospital to see these recordings because I knew a doctor there—and was able to see them confidentially. I saw a schizophrenic there in full crisis, a guy who was a grad from a major business school, a brilliant guy who said: "I am crazy because when I talk I see shapes coming out of my mouth; I see beings around people. I know they don't exist, therefore I am crazy." At the time I saw this recording I told myself: "This guy's really cracked."

Coming back from Peru, I thought about this poor guy and said to myself: "If this guy was with the Indians, they would get him back together straightaway. He is someone who can see things we can't."

VINCENT: I can only half agree with you here because what specifically allows you to get it back together after an experience like this is the fact that you are well balanced, mentally. If you are a schizophrenic front and back, ultimately this makes zero plus zero equals Toto's noggin.* Where is someone who is a schizophrenic going to go to get it together? He takes ayahuasca, he has a split personality, and when he comes back he has a split personality. That's going to happen as the Indians say; he is going to go into the world of the spirits, and he is going to stay there.

I have people around me who have been schizophrenic for a long

---

*[Toto's noggin is a child's drawing of a round head in which all the features are a stylized representation of the math equation 0 + 0 = 0. —*Trans.*]

time, so it's a problem I am quite familiar with, and I don't really know if it helps to make it easier to enter the spirit world, but in everyday life, it is going to make things worse.

JAN: I agree with you. There are people who have come and told me: "A person I know is schizophrenic," and I have never said to go to the jungle. I have always told them: "It is double or nothing." But I've thought to myself that maybe, when he learns there might only be two other people in the same reality, he'll no longer tell himself: "What I am experiencing is madness because I am the only one in my culture who experiences it."

VINCENT: Well, that's different. When someone, who for reason X, has a more perceptive system than usual and you have him discuss it with people who have had shamanic experiences and they tell him: "What you are seeing might be a materialization of this, or an energy that you are feeling, et cetera," and they discuss it with him, I think that this could be rather a good thing—a way of accompanying someone through schizophrenia as a support for guiding him in a different way through what we call "madness." This is something that can work with a certain category of schizophrenics. But having someone take ayahuasca who is already in that state naturally, just what more will that do for him?

JAN: I don't know; I'm no doctor.

VINCENT: Would you tell someone standing at the edge of a cliff: "Jump, it's not dangerous"?

JAN: That's an artist's hypothesis. . . .

VINCENT: I know cases where the result was not conclusive.

JAN: You have witnessed schizophrenics taking it.

VINCENT: Not ayahuasca, but iboga.

JAN: Things did not go well?

VINCENT: No, things did not go at all well. Mainly because one of them ended up in the psychiatric word of a Gabon hospital, and then had to be repatriated. Although iboga is more likely than ayahuasca to fix you. If you want to look at it another way, iboga is really quite structural and appears to you one thought after the other; it is not like ayahuasca where you take off into things. . . .

JEREMY: From what you have been saying, in the final analysis, there has been a lot of damage done by iboga.

VINCENT: Frankly, I don't know. It's very complicated, certainly just like everything about Africa can be complicated. I am not especially paranoid. My experience was truly brilliant, so if I am so determined to apply the brakes to this thing, it is because I have my reasons. No, the return in this is not favorable today. It is as clear as that.

JEREMY: Could you say that ayahuasca was cooler than iboga?

VINCENT: I've had less contact with people who take ayahuasca because I have not written a book on it. Furthermore, ayahuasca is now very well organized. Iboga, well iboga is still African, and Africa is a bit unique.

JEREMY: Did less corpses pile up with ayahuasca?

VINCENT: I've seen people flip their lids, but as I mention on *Nouvelles du Monde entier* [News from the Whole World], things remained good-natured.

But to return to the question of healing, what has this brought to you as a self-healing process? I am talking physically. . . .

JEREMY: In any case, Lévi-Strauss said in 1949 that Westerners could comprehend shamanism in terms of psychotherapy. Psychotherapy had already been in existence for fifty years when he wrote this. Western culture had just rediscovered this matter. So that connection is something that is already on the table.

For me personally as a fairly healthy guy, I go there not for healing but to learn things. In the indigenous context, young people use the plants that teach them how to find their life path. It is extremely common. A number of contemporary indigenous adults have told me:

"I went through this initiation, I saw my life path, and everything I saw came true." As for those who told me: "I saw all sorts of things and none came true," there was not a single person.

Personally, my own experience is interrogating the ayahuasca sphere, guided by an indigenous shaman, about my life path: "What should I think about what I've done to this point? Starting here, what should I do during the months to come? Show me, if you please, what I need to know. . . ."

And these are often complex threads; they give you angles and points of view. In one session, I saw myself through the eyes of my son: in my vision I leave my office at the end of the day, somewhat preoccupied with my intellectual stories, and I am several feet taller than he is; and in fact Dad is off in a world of his own. And from what I was able to see through his eyes was that I was in the process of letting the childhood of my children pass me by, caught up in my business, while they were the really important thing. So this really gave me the taste of talking to them by bringing myself down to their own physical level and listening to them. "Okay, now you have to come out of your thing and you are with them, so listen."

VINCENT: That is a very good example because you have clearly summed up the process of positive psychology. This is a typical thing provided by ayahuasca, this kind of vision that completely simplifies things.

JEREMY: Once you have seen it you cannot un-see it or erase it, and so you know it! And this transforms how you conduct yourself in the world—constructively.

VINCENT: Absolutely, yes.

JEREMY: I learned things about how to be with my children and with my parents, how to accompany my parents, who are more anchored in the twentieth century, and more like Westerners, and who, well, have to deal with Western medicine. Everyone has got to deal at one time or another with his parents at the end of their lives, and his children, if he is lucky enough to have any.

You can visit a psychotherapist or a counselor, but I have found that consulting a good Amazonian shaman is very helpful. . . . You go there with your little question, you go through the session, and then, the next day, you talk with the shaman. You say: "Listen, during the session I saw this, and in the meantime, here is the subject that concerns me. What can you say about it?" These individuals can be a source of incredible wisdom and at the same time have a staggering simplicity.

VINCENT: Often ayahuasca trips are very, very strong; you go off into things that have very little relationship to our everyday reality. But there is a moment when you can really make good use of it, for things concerning your life path or everyday life: it is the specific moment when you are coming down from this trip. You have not yet come back completely to "real" life, and you are no longer on that kind of extremely strong cosmic journey.

I find that this is a moment when reflection is particularly sharp, where you have access to a kind of synthesized reflection in which you can find an answer about a vision or an impression. I think you have described this extremely well: all at once seeing yourself as bigger than your son. This is of such basic simplicity, and it is true that there you have access to a capacity of intelligence that is quite noticeable: I don't know if it is like that for you.

JAN: You could say: "Do you need ayahuasca for this?" Perhaps some people need to be hit with a club? After a while, integration occurs when very simple aspects of life have been changed.

You shall discover it by quite simply realizing that you have entered into another rhythm, things like that. It is often territories that demand a lot of our attention, simple things like presence. Don't do two things at the same time—thinking about a new novel, a new film, while doing the dishes, even. Think about what you are doing. You are guided in here by simple and direct relationships, not by things at the far ends of the universe, nor the great mysteries. It is in little things that you find the essential. After all, the everyday life is your life.

JEREMY: I don't know if this concurs with your experience, but the

Ashaninca shaman who was my informant stressed one thing: say what I do and do what I say. Make the words that come out of your mouth conform with your actions. This is the proof that you are a serious individual. From the shamanic point of view, words can heal. They are connected with knowledge and power.

Doing this, you have to pay attention to what comes out of your mouth. If you don't want shit coming out of your mouth, well, then don't say the word. And using the same logic, it would instead involve creating stories that have a happy ending if you want to see constructive things happening in the world. It is true that this makes protesting all that much harder—in any case it comes down to measuring each word. After being conscientious in this regard, you will realize that you also create the world. The world exists outside of us, but we form part of a continuing creation, we are creatures that create symbols and who make meaning, and as a result of what we emit into the world, the world changes.

Therefore, what I write, what I say, every word is of extreme importance. So it is easy to see how when you return to Europe with this point of view and you see people who say just anything and who are aggressive—it is difficult to find common ground for understanding. I think that contact with shamans can teach you to speak more precisely, and at the same time, this can make it harder to live in a commercial world with its constant messages.

JAN: During my last journey, I went through a very strong moment during a session. I cannot talk about the vision, because it is very hard to put into words, but I saw, or thought I saw quite clearly, that the world resembled what we thought. This is only a philosophical idea: an interrelationship between our thoughts and physical reality. We think a world, and the world thinks itself and it is us. The result is something quite beautiful; this was wonderment, followed, quite suddenly, by profound sorrow in the face of what we've made of it. I wept in fact.

I wept, but I stiffened my upper lip, gritted my teeth, and let things flow, without grabbing hold of the thought, the sorrow; otherwise I think I would have collapsed into the deepest depression. And then, afterward, joy came, and surrender.

What you say reminded me of this: pay attention to what you think, because when you express it, it is going to go to work in the world, and it is going to become a gesture, thus an action. Try to establish consistency between your thought and your actions. The warrior's action is to pay attention to your thought and your action, and at the same time keep an eye on its emotional dimension.

JEREMY: I also like what this Ashaninca shaman said about handling alcohol in the form of manioc beer. In fact just about everyone has a canoe filled with manioc beer every day. It is slightly alcoholic, and if you fill up on it, you will get drunk. And he said that someone who was drunk on manioc beer and began talking like this: "I am going to build a house over there," if tomorrow he got up and began concretely putting into practice what he said when he was drunk, then he did not have a drinking problem. [Laughs.] If, on the other hand, when he drinks and talks like that, and then the next day: "Oh, I have a bit of a headache; no, today I am not going to do anything," and does not honor his drunkenness, then he really does have an alcohol problem.

This means that the reason to work hard during the day and do what you said you would do is to be able to drink again in the evening [laughs]; you drink hard and you work hard, and that's a place you can go. It is hygienic to do what you say when you are drunk; or else stop drinking.

JAN: It is true that intoxication with alcohol is interesting—any kind of intoxication is interesting, because it is going to awaken a lot of things. I observe the people who have drunk, who smoked grass.

JEREMY: Yeah, "Tomorrow I'm going to change the world!"

JAN: In fact, I am not going to judge the person, but I am going to learn a lot of things that are going to help me weave my relationship with him or her. For example, if someone begins to let loose with a lot of vulgar idiocies that are slightly racist, dimwitted, or sexual, I am going to tell myself: "Wait a minute, he feels at home with this." It is not the alcohol; the alcohol is only having a liberating effect.

Paradoxically it is the opposite sometimes; you have someone who is very shy that starts talking, it's magnificent. But all at once, you are going to say: "There's something hidden here. It is a shame that this happens with alcohol; he or she should look for another way to let it out."

We, in our culture—and I find this crazy—when someone has been really odious because he has been drinking, people say: "But he had been drinking, it is the alcohol. . . ."

JEREMY: It's scandalous!

VINCENT: We are entering another debate here, but I am not really so sure that alcohol does any good. It might be revealing at times, certainly. But at the same time, someone who gets sloshed every day is revealing his bad side all the time.

JEREMY: You take the millions of people who drink, you take the 10 or 20 percent of them who are alcoholics, and then you take the percentage who beat their wives. And you take the corpses left by car accidents. . . . These are statistics in fact. Then you take iboga, for example, line up the corpses, and make the comparison.

What I find remarkable all the same with alcohol is that you have almost 80 percent of the population, tens, hundreds of millions of people in the world who can drink more or less in good humor, communication, and friendship, and without brawls or fistfights.

VINCENT: There was an interesting show on public television channel "Arte," *Drugs and the Brain,* and the expert said that alcohol was really serious. But fine, I'm not really objective about this subject. I do not like alcohol. I find it makes people moronic.

JEREMY: That's the problem with alcohol: one or two glasses of good Bordeaux a day—

JAN: One or two glasses of good Bordeaux a day, that's a good thing!

JEREMY: An Ashaninca shaman that I met told me: "El cuerpo mecessita su licor cada día." The body needs its liquor every day.

VINCENT: Dear friends, we have gone astray from our subject. I would like to add a small detail concerning healing. . . .

JEREMY: There is something I wanted to say about healing.

VINCENT: Go on.

JEREMY: A shaman I know stepped on the trip wire of a hunter's trap when gathering plants in the jungle and took a volley of grapeshot at point-blank range that broke his tibia. He was brought to the hospital after having lost a lot of blood. He was given a blood transfusion and some screws were put in. He was given some antibiotics and sent home. Then he continued to treat himself with plants. There's nothing like two to three nuts and bolts and a few antibiotics for a case like this, even for a great shaman.

VINCENT: I could give the same testimony. For a major injury, I don't think we should delude ourselves, shamanism will not be able to work. The proof: all the shamans I know have had more or less extensive stays in the hospital.

On the other hand, based on what I've been able to observe, because I've gone through all these initiations, because I have a fairly strict life hygienically, and having better management of my brain and body, that in fact I never have any minor ailments. All those things like colds, grippe, sore throats . . .

Like any city dweller, I regularly feel like I'm coming down with a sore throat, with a cold. There are people around me who are sick, but I never catch anything. I have really learned to maintain an inner economy that ensures I never catch these kinds of things.

On the other hand, I had a fairly powerful virus that turned out to be hepatitis C. I worked on it with ayahuasca. I had visions about my hepatitis C. I think this helped, but it did not prevent the fact that I ended up following a good old chemotherapy treatment, and thanks to that, for the moment, the virus is gone, which is not the case with the traditional medicines.

Energetically rebalancing yourself, learning to manage things better, is all very good. I believe it is good to form intersections with modern medicine, but it is necessary to avoid being naive in regard to it.

I believe there are people with very advanced states of illness, at the terminal stage, and who at a particular time refuse to follow treatments that might have cured them, telling themselves: "There is going to be a miracle remedy that will cure me," and this can have tragic consequences.

JAN: I have seen people with very serious diseases, which can be treated, but who are given a death sentence by doctors, who have gone down there in search of a cure, and why not?

JEREMY: You have seen them?

JAN: Yes, actually . . . whose condition has stabilized. Especially for autoimmune diseases: things like multiple sclerosis, that kind of thing.

VINCENT: Stabilized . . . ?

JAN: There was no remission of the disease, and the person was not cured. But she had been given six months to live; that was three years ago and the condition has stabilized. I know that this person says: "Ah! It's starting up again. I must go back there."

VINCENT: Just who is this, is it . . . ?

JAN: No, you don't know this person. But him, too—I think you are thinking of the same person I am—his condition has stabilized.

There are diseases that our medicine still has a problem treating, a little like cancer twenty years ago, which is no longer the case today. It is even fairly effective on certain cancers; the progress made by medicine is incredible. You see, these are illnesses you inflict upon yourself, unconsciously; it is an inner system. But on the viral and infectious aspect, our medicine is much more effective.

So I have become a reverse shaman. I went to a community one day where a kid had an infection. He had a lump. You see it, you say: "Good, I am going to give him an aspirin. He is twelve—perhaps an aspirin cut in half."

The next day, there was nothing there. He had never taken aspirin in his life. You see, it is like pure magic for certain things.

So, for psychological disorders, in any case a little depression, some relationship problems—I agree with you about schizophrenics. And things that we have trouble treating.

Depression is something we treat by creating chemical barriers that prevent the people from becoming immersed in their problems. Whereas plants force you to dive straight into the heart of your problem, and the shaman is there to hold you up and help you through it.

It's obvious: if I have an infection, I will go straight to the hospital. But I believe I would try both together a little. Prepare myself with ayahuasca, go under the knife, then go back there.

There is not one medicine that is better than the other; there are things that may be more effective in certain domains, and others that are more effective in others.

But I am a little like you. When I was younger—this comes with age, perhaps—I was always sick. Starting from the moment that ayahuasca gives you a perception of your body, something happens. Quite simply, you are better. Here I am forty-three years old, and I am better than I was at twenty or thirty.

JEREMY: Let's say you are in the Amazon jungle, there is no hospital nearby, and you become seriously ill. I think that having a ritualized shamanic session to call the spirits to help you could be useful. . . . There is some hocus-pocus in shamanism, for example, making the patient see things that he thinks are a priori impossible. This action seems to trigger self-healing energies in people.

VINCENT: You mean to say, you take the illness and then—

JEREMY: Yes, I take out the stones and then we perform a ceremony. We accompany you on the journey within, we put all our strength into it, and something magic happens. And the simple fact of doing something rather than nothing can help trigger the body's self-healing abilities.

VINCENT: That's something that is sure and certain.

JEREMY: Why deprive yourself of it, in fact?

JAN: I went back this summer to shoot a film on maternal health. So, for a while in the Shipibo communities I was only talking with the midwives, with women, about what it was like to have a child, to give birth, to go to the hospital. I went to the hospital, I met the doctors, I saw the women. And, my God, what violence!

You have to realize the problem: there is one woman out of a thousand in the West who dies from creating a new life; there are thirty in the underdeveloped countries. But in the Amazon the rate soars. In every family there is a woman who died, like it was in our villages at the beginning of the twentieth century. My grandmother died in labor, a long time ago. When there was hemorrhaging, there was not much a doctor could do.

So you go there and you realize how terrible this is. I am not saying: "How well off we are in our cities, close to our hospitals," but it is something that we have. And when you have it, well, you have a desire to look for more essential things . . . but you see people facing things that are super tough. I did not think it would be so violent. For certain things, we in our world do a good job.

If you had an ambulance that went from the hospital to the port, in Pucallpa—because women arrive in the middle of giving birth after a four-hour boat ride. There are no cars so they get into motorized rickshaws and they arrive—they are dead when they get to the hospital. And you say to yourself: "They don't even have the funds to take care of this." So you think about the other side of our world.

JEREMY: What the shaman knows is how to treat the individual. In contrast, I've had several recent experiences with European surgery in which the patients were treated like objects to be repaired.

And I am sure that the healing of people would be accelerated and facilitated if hospitals had a more human touch. I have the impression that doctors deliberately look at their patients with a cold eye because there are so many—the hospital operates on an industrial scale—and they must not let themselves get emotionally involved.

VINCENT: That said, things are in the process of improving.

JAN: But it is true that on the human level, it is terrible.

VINCENT: I find that a lot of progress has been made in ten years. Before when you were in the wing for children, you were not allowed to spend the night; now there are beds. I find that the medical system in France is extremely effective in its own sphere.

JEREMY: It is true that the nurses and the ambulance personnel are often wonderful. But I am talking about the doctor himself, the healer who comes in wearing his white robe. He has a tendency to be cold and distant, and to talk like a specialist. But why take the human element out of the therapeutic, medical, surgical relationship?

VINCENT: That is the problem of compartmentalization. It is perhaps what differentiates a shamanic system that tries to re-situate a being. . . .

JAN: No, because I can talk to you about doctors in India—when I made the film about Amma, who built hospitals in India for the poor. You see, at the hospital, they are working in devotion and in a human environment. If I had to go to the hospital, I would prefer to go Amma's hospital in India. It is the exact opposite: they are there to help human beings. They are more connected to a spiritual being, to a spirituality.

So I think that this is a question of culture and education. You can be educated about the technological aspect of the human being and repair him from a physical standpoint without having to be in a dehumanized system. It is not because you have learned to fix something like a piece of meat that it is only a piece of meat. You look in the person's body, and then when the time comes you look at the person.

JEREMY: It should be noted that what is absent in our culture is the strength of shamans. So, how do we make it possible to grasp the therapeutic effectiveness of shamans, as this is what we are lacking?

It would be interesting to combine their way with ours, to show some humility and say we don't know everything. We could combine our ways of knowing and healing people, connect both methods, if people wanted to.

JAN: A convention of doctors should be organized for them to take ayahuasca.

VINCENT: If you were the Minister of Health, right. . . . [Laughs.]

MICHKA: As a reader, I would like to ask you if you have the impression that a shamanic experience can be colored by the fact that the shaman is a man or a woman, and the conclusions that might flow out of this. . . .

VINCENT: I am going to give a very macho answer: I have always been initiated by men. In Gabon. The initiation of men and women is not . . .

JAN: They are not mixed?

VINCENT: They are not mixed, no; and I was initiated by a man in Peru. Women have a specific quality, but I only know this because someone told me not because I experienced it personally. This is only because there is a difference between men and women; each represents a different sensibility.

From what I've felt personally as an outside observer, women's role is not the same as men's; but I think that shamanism is made up of relatively technical and down-to-earth principles in which everything has a useful role, basic principles that are the male principle and the female principle. That is true for the two traditions I've experienced. Based on what I know, in archaic traditions women initiated women. There were secrets passed on woman to woman in the same way that a man can be initiated as a warrior or hunter (this does not mean that a woman cannot be a warrior or a hunter).

Some of these things can still be seen if you go back several generations. Men and women are two distinct things . . . they don't perform the same activities, their lives are not formatted the same way. I think it was Jeremy who once said that women had problems with shamanic sessions, that it was hard for them to go bury themselves in the jungle when they had their periods, or even practical problems because, with children, it's not always easy. . . . But it would be hard for me to say more about this to you.

JAN: The impression I've had is that first there is a great complicity in the maloca during the rituals, person to person, and at times there are discussions, laughter shared by men and women. The therapist is really doing group work.

I've seen situations where women have guided the ceremonies, or else it was two women and a man, like one of the sessions with Guillermo, when he invited a Shipibo female shaman, Olivia Arevalo, who was known in the region and came from Juventus San Rafael. He did not sing a song; he was facing her. And I can say there was something physical going on there.

It was something quite tender. It smacked of true healing, of the heart, of love, despite the very intense visions. And this woman was a warrior; more of light and heart I would say than knowledge. There was something of that nature emanating from her. I only went through one session with her—but I looked for her, I went back so I could resume working with her.

So, I think that women have a heart in Shipibo shamanism. They are not necessarily pushed into the spotlight when foreigners are around, but they still have something quite strong and specific, which doesn't seem so different from men's knowledge.

When the shaman is looking out for you, if he tells you: "This evening I want you to take ayahuasca with this person," you should tell yourself: "He is giving you a gift and an invitation, and you are going to learn something this evening." This stage is perfectly consistent with your prior experience with this individual who is passing things on to you—and who at a given point is going to share the pure and strong feminine energy of a great woman healer with you.

Okay, there are things having to do with women; when they have their periods they cannot take ayahuasca, nor be in the maloca, things like that. . . . But that's all.

JEREMY: I believe that the Shipibo are a little unique in the sense where, in things touching on the shamanic sphere, women have a greater importance there than among neighboring peoples in the region. That said, it is true that Amazonian shamanism has been especially studied by male anthropologists, who have a tendency to focus on the masculine; so, you could say that indigenous female ayahuasca shamanism is not even close to being fully studied. Or maybe there is not as much of it as we would like.

You have to realize that at least 90 percent of the ayahuasqueros are men, so you have nine out of ten chances to be initiated by a man. It is also true that when I lived with the Ashaninca, if the anthropologist spent the day with the women, it was not viewed well. The men were active in the forest and the women kept busy in the gardens and the home, and the men would not leave for the jungle and leave me alone with the women.

That said, the rare times when I've had the pleasure of being in the presence of a woman ayahuasca shaman, it was with Maria Valera, Guillermo's mother, who was over eighty years old, and what I would identify with this experience was the songs—she goes much higher. It was exceptional; it caused the hair to stand up on your head. It was stratospheric snake-charming music. The interweaving of the male voice and the female voice is a marvel.

And among the Shipibo, the women are artisans and create all those labyrinths on their textiles and pottery, which they look for in their visions. . . . It is the women who render what is seen in the world of visions concrete.

I think there is a way to put this question more precisely. You must ask yourself about any shaman, whether a man or a woman: Is he a good plumber or a bad plumber? Is she a good shaman or a bad shaman? This comes back to the question: How is his or her singing? This is the core of the matter; shamans are first and foremost singers, and whatever a shaman does, he makes music, says Gilbert Rouget in *Music and Trance*.

So, do you prefer male or female singers? There are fewer female singers than male singers, but I should say that there are several women singers who do things to me that the male singers do not. When you have that female voice that enchants you—it is more refined, subtle, it has more grace. And it is true that in men's energy you will have a tendency to have that energy of the hunter, the predator, a little more frontal.

This does not mean there are no witches. I think that women, when they go to the dark side, can be just as destructive as men.

I knew two shamanesses who use San Pedro cactus in the Chiclayo area, and these women had a mischievous side. They were little women who sparkled all over and had a side that was a little maternal and a little bit playful. They did not take themselves too seriously. They had a lighter manner, while we men are maybe more caught up in power struggles.

JAN: There is something else—because there are two parts to your question. What is the connection with sex as well, perhaps?

Are we of the same sex or of the opposite sex? This works on energies that are also energies of desire, sexual energies. Ayahuasca is not an aphrodisiac. But the body is there, too. That means when you start exploring your body, you are going to rediscover things concerning sensuality and desire. And when you are in these active domains and a woman singing for a man is facing you, some things are going to be established with or between you.

We have talked quite a bit about suffering; but physical ecstasy exists, too. Once the fears racing through you relax into your body, a perfectly symmetrical ecstasy follows in their wake. It is the songs that take you there; and this is where I see a difference. I think when a male shaman sings for a woman, additional forces come into play, forces that are going to stoke up the man-and-woman aspect of their relationship.

You see, if the woman healer who sang for me was only half her age at the time—she was eighty—then I'm not sure what might have happened, because it was so strong. . . .

She brought something into play, and I gave it back because she was touching on things like ecstasy, even love; I couldn't take any more in, I couldn't take any more.

The time will come when you will say to yourself while remembering this experience, "This person made me feel this emotion."

JEREMY: She enchanted you.

JAN: She enchanted me. It so happens that I adore this woman; she is a person who is important to me—my last film bears her name. But, there are levels of complicity that can be even more incredible, I think.

Last but not least, there are problems of desire and love.

JEREMY: Let's say that there is clearly a tension between the fact that actually when a male shaman sings over a female client, he will enchant her as much as he will enchant a man, but this implies that he has a power over her and there are all sorts of cases of indigenous shamans sleeping with the charming Western women passing through, who are absolutely enchanted about sleeping with their shaman.

And between adults, as far as I'm concerned, everyone can do what they want as long as it is between consenting adults, but . . . generally speaking, it is not a good idea to sleep with your therapist. I am sure that everyone agrees on this, psychotherapists, psychoanalysts, everyone. And it is appropriate to talk about this to everyone's clients, the clients of psychotherapists and shamans. . . . Warning, warning!

JAN: This is no longer the case among the Shipibo, but traditionally men could have two or three wives; and the shamans had twenty, who were from all the villages. So if you want to forewarn people of what they might run in to: "Pay attention to this particular danger, or this particular thing."

It is not dangerous for desire to arise when you are with someone and they are with you. What is dangerous is the relationship that you are going to make out of this if you believe the person is a kind of extremely profound traditional sage.

I have often told the young women I see in the jungle, who are quite pretty: "By the way, if you visit the Indians, the shamans, you should know that even with someone who has really gotten you worked up one night, you can always say no!" And they say: "But if I refuse, he will stop treating me." I know a few stories like that.

It is said that it is never good to sleep with your therapist. But that's our vision, for shamanism. . . . I have never had the opportunity to test it, so I don't know; I have to try it someday with a woman healer! [Laughs.]

I had to laugh when you said: "You should not sleep with your therapist." Wait, that is the very first rule. I believe it is necessary to have good, clear, simple, direct relationships, one human being to another.

VINCENT: What's more in this kind of dimension, the notion of sexual polarity may disappear. Ultimately, you are not resonating at all with the sexual. Not that it has been disassociated but—

JEREMY: You don't want to be a spoilsport but—

VINCENT: In this instance, personally, I have the tendency rather to do my fucking on the ground and to go up when I go up. At the same time, I think there are people whose initiation includes sexuality. A shaman might pass things on to someone because he feels closer to him. Then, I also basically think that the majority of people are not true shamans. There are people who often use their small powers to go too far. I know of women who were half raped in Pucallpa by pseudo-shamans.

It is true when you go to Pucallpa, and it is true in any country; it was true in India during the 1970s with the fake gurus. . . . This is something we haven't touched on yet. We are here because we, we were lucky to meet master initiators who are true shamans. We managed to find all this. But there are lots of people who land in these kinds of places, who get to the airport . . . just like me, I, too, have roamed around a lot of countries saying: "Hi there! Here I am, I am clueless about this place; I am looking for a shaman."

The result is really enlightening. You have some real shamans but you also have the fake shamans, the charlatans, the ill-intentioned people, a little bit of everything. So, it is not because the people are shamans that they are necessarily great guys. It might be a good idea to add a small heading: "How to do it? Who to seek out?" Because that's a big part of this picture, too.

And getting back to the sex thing, it is true that it sometimes sticks out like a sore thumb that the shaman is fucking the Westerners who come to him. . . . After all, it's a question of what his own intentions are thereby—are they good or not? Can it hurt a person's development? Frankly, I don't know. What do you think about it?

JEREMY: The bottom line right now indicates that it is rather disturbing. In any case, during a session, indigenous wisdom states that is to be squarely avoided.

JAN: I spoke earlier about a woman healer. . . .You feel things during the ceremony, but they are things that might translate into states and enthusiasms six hours later, when you have returned into your body.

JEREMY: What an Ashaninca shaman told me . . . I had asked him: "Some people say that after an ayahuasca session, you should abstain for a certain period." And he said: "No, as long as it is with your wife, it's all right." That means the main thing is love. If it is making love with the one you love, and with whom you have a deepening relationship, it is not problematic. So, it is not the sex act itself, it is how it is done, with whom it is done, and in what spirit it is done. On the one hand—and on the other—it is true that there are dangers lurking when someone takes part in an ayahuasca session. When people you do not know are sleeping in the dark next to you . . .

JAN: And all at once you have a wave of love for the girl next to you. . . .

JEREMY: Yes, this kind of thing happens regularly, and it is mentioned often. It is not necessarily bad that people fall in love with each other, but I think all the same that you still have to be aware that you are exposing yourself to . . .

JAN: . . . bad surprises.

JEREMY: This is not trivial. There is a book by a physicist named Fred Alan Wolf in which he tells his personal story. He fell madly in love with a young twenty-year-old Peruvian girl during an ayahuasca session. He stopped thinking about quantum physics and became obsessed with his Dulcinea, and you can read it. . . . [Laughs.] He writes with remarkable honesty and then, in the end, he realizes that she was not who he thought she was. An emotional disaster courtesy of ayahuasca.

JAN: Ayahuasca couples; that's not a bad way to get things stirred up. I've seen a lot of couples go there, and in fact, it has not worked out. But me, for example, with Anne, my companion—our love story was born with the vine seven years ago. It's a very beautiful story, a little girl was born. . . . So this is a territory of meeting, separation, in short, of movement.

JEREMY: It can help transform you.

JAN: It changes you. . . . But there are couples consisting of people who get along well together. It can also strengthen relationships.

JEREMY: In any case, it is a delicate matter. You hear shamans say that the more they gain in experience the less they consume hallucinogens. And the older you grow and you have a little more knowledge about it, the less you need to go there, for example, if you are a couple. And then, if from time to time you want to share an experience together, this does not mean that you have to do it together all the time. . . . Once again, everyone can do what they like, but speaking frankly, when you are young, you go through phases. Sometimes, you need to have intense and repeated experiences, but mastery of the thing takes place at a certain distance. [Laughs.]

JAN: I find that the plant is a lover. There is something feminine about ayahuasca. It is a siren. There is a love story—but an amazing one.

I was offered the chance to have a session with iboga and at the time I was curious. One night, I was taking part in an ayahuasca ceremony and a moment came—I had gone into the world of visions—when I clearly had, or thought I had, a message. The plant spoke to me of what I was going to do. In the form of very pretty waves . . . But it was something along the lines of communication.

I had heard stories about the jealousy of plants, and there was something like that here, that said: "Listen, we have good communication and are getting along well. If you go with someone else, you are going to have another kind of communication. You are free to do it but you are going to break what we have together. Is this what you really want?"

So then I, the bashful lover, said: "No, no," I canceled the rendezvous with iboga, and now I am vigilantly weaving a beautiful love relationship with ayahuasca. If I am telling this story, it is just out of respect for love, desire. . . .

We see that this plant is intelligent. When it enters into contact with you, there are two of you. Sometimes she gives me a very unsexy spanking over a trifle, but she loves me and I love her.

VINCENT: I realize that I am a bit more Cartesian—with Jesuit tendencies, of course. [Laughs.] I really have a different kind of conceptual system. It is true that I never took that position with iboga or with ayahuasca. That's the kind of relationship I would share with the Earth, for example, with this global entity that is the Earth, for which all these plants and learning are an expression. This is more the kind of relationship I would have with the planet. But with ayahuasca itself? No, I have never seen it as a . . .

JAN: A feminine symbol, a lover.

VINCENT: Neither feminine nor masculine, no. I don't think ayahuasca is binary, for example—anyway that's what I think—whereas the male-female principle is a binary principle. But I could be wrong.

The charm of these kinds of experiences is that it makes you feel the complexity and multiplicity of things. No one point of view is right; what matters is how it resonates inside; the reality of things is right there. And I think that it is the addition of all these points of view that makes a point of view true. Right?

JAN: I have the impression that it is feminine, but feminine doesn't mean it's a woman. I have the impression that during the relationship, something is stimulated in how you feel. The only other time this feeling is stimulated is when you're with a lover. A level has been activated, one connected to desire, to something organic but something beautiful. It's an amorous feeling, but with the body. Now, she also forces me to look at things green and unripened. . . .

JEREMY: Let's say the subject is the secret garden, and talking about one's ayahuasca experiences is a little like talking about one's sexual experiences. It is very intimate, it is intense, it is a little embarrassing and . . . it's taboo, in fact. So, it is a little along the same lines. Because it's the secret garden.

VINCENT: It's very interesting what you just said.

JEREMY: And for a heterosexual guy, it will evoke the encounter. . . .

JAN: That's it!

JEREMY: There are a lot of people, indigenous ones included, who say that the spirit of ayahuasca is feminine. . . . It is true that the intelligence that regularly speaks to me in the ayahuasca state always makes me think of an old Chinese sage.

It is basically not really a man or a woman. It is just old and wise, and plant and human, a subtle feeling that is also sensual . . .

JAN: I am with you when you say that it is an old Chinese sage speaking into your ear sometimes, or the mythological serpent who looks you in the eyes and who shows you. But sometimes this old sage is going to transform into . . . something that includes desire, love; which includes physical desire. For me it is one of the facets.

[Silence.]

VINCENT: Great, my friends, have a good weekend.

TIGRANE: I would like to raise one final little question and your answer can be only one syllable: it is easy to imagine that there are some things people don't talk about because they are forbidden to. Are there any things you aren't talking about because they are taboo for you?

VINCENT: Yes, this is very clear to me. In my initiations I've had things communicated to me that are unspeakable for reasons of secrecy, and I respect traditions. There is something fairly paradoxical about this as many "secrets" can be found in esoteric bookstores: and others can't be found there, on the other hand, and remain unspeakable. That's my answer.

JAN: No, I have the impression that there are no secrets in Shipibo shamanism, or no secrets in the sense we give that word. On the other hand, there are things that are hard to talk about, either because you have accepted that you are unable to communicate this particular thing, or because you are venturing into territories that, in comparison with what you already know, are going to make you feel uncomfortable. When you start talking about the subject, your body starts sending you signals you shouldn't be going there. It's not that I don't want to talk about it, it's that all at once the thought flies off and the body starts to keep watch over it. Some things you're not going to talk about but not because you don't have the right to talk about them; anyway, that's how it is with the Shipibo, you just avoid discussing them.

VINCENT: I was initiated in Gabon, which is a French-speaking country. Luckily, I speak French. But when I am traveling, I don't have any contact through language, no verbal communication in fact, except in Gabon. I was initiated into the Bwiti, and in fact there are few Bwiti members in Gabon. It is a small category of the population, I suppose equivalent to Freemasons in France. They have fairly strict rules all the same: when you are in kindergarten you have to respect this thing, in elementary school, you should respect that thing, when you have had an initiation like this, this corresponds to that thing—which I think exists among the Shipibo and the Ashaninca, but at a less profound level. In Gabon I had this kind of initiation. So, I was told: "This is something you must never talk about; that is something you cannot talk about to women." After you have been initiated into a tradition, you play the game.

And the Shipibo thing is not secret but is more along the lines of the unspeakable. That is to say it serves no purpose to talk about it, for the simple reason that in their communication system there is no point in talking about things that have no equivalence. In conclusion, finally, the sole conceptual tools that have really helped me to try to explain the experience—although I don't have any scientific training whatsoever—are what I've found in science, mainly in what I know of quantum physics, astrophysics, and things like that. Otherwise it is fairly difficult, apart from poetry or art, to have a system and a language to explain it.

JAN: Concerning secrecy, there was an excellent epigraph from Benny Shanon at the beginning of his book *The Antipodes of the Mind*. He told a story that someone had told him in Pucallpa. In it he says that when God created the universe, he wanted to make a place to put all the secrets of creation. He told himself that he should put them somewhere on the planet Earth, where the people who found the secrets would be capable of using them without destroying everything. So, he said he would hide them in the depths of the ocean. This way, only men capable of constructing machines and manufacturing a reality strong enough to get to the bottom of the ocean would find these secrets; but in fact, they would not be good men. So he thought of the moon, but it was the same story. And the story could have kept going, but finally God had an idea. He decided to put all the secrets of the universe at the bottom of the mind and heart of every human being. This way, whoever could find the path leading to the bottom of his mind and heart would find them.

VINCENT: That's a very nice story.

Okay, listen. . . . The time is still not right yet for me to get all holier than thou—I am definitely the namby-pamby spoilsport of the gathering. . . .

JAN: We are going to keep going after you split, we're going to smoke, we're going to talk about you behind your back. [Laughs.]

VINCENT: . . . Okay fine, it is half past midnight. We've talked a lot.

Someone should perhaps put together a first transcription, and we can see a little of what might be missing, or what is not working. Once this is done, we could do a second complementary session. . . . No? What do you think?

JEREMY: Shall we bleep each other?

VINCENT: That's right, let's bleep each other. But getting back to this, excuse me again [laughs], but we have to keep something in mind: Are we making a book on ayahuasca or not? You see, putting the vine in the title is still making it on ayahuasca. . . . Afterward, it is really an editorial decision.

MICHKA: At the same time, if we remove it, what are we talking about?

TIGRANE: And also at the same time, the subject is not only ayahuasca. . . .

VINCENT: The subject that interests me personally is much larger. I find that ayahuasca is a bit reductive. . . .

JAN: I do not think we have been reducing things.

TIGRANE: I have the impression that ayahuasca is more like a common territory the three of you share that gives you the opportunity to speak about profound and mysterious things. What would be some other common points you share that let you speak about what lies beyond . . . ?

JAN: Yes, that makes a lot of things in common, in fact! [Laughs.]

JEREMY: I think we are modest: we are not claiming to be other than who we are: individual people with limited experience. We have trajectories that are necessarily subjective and personal, and we are not claiming to be the world's greatest authorities on the subject. It is just a conversation, a long conversation about our encounter with shamanism.

JAN: All the same we have talked a lot about ayahuasca.

VINCENT: This is not necessarily an impediment; it is also a matter of what the title will be.

JEREMY: And what we have learned from mingling with these peoples in Africa and the Amazon, with their plants. . . .

JAN: The word *ayahuasca* has to be in it. In any event, it is the source. . . . Otherwise, where are we? We're not philosophers, you know.

TIGRANE: The basic theme is not ayahuasca; it is teaching plants, states of altered consciousness. . . .

VINCENT: But no matter how many times we repeat: "It is not a drug, it is not this or that," 99 percent of people get confused.

JEREMY: It is also the attempt to make a lively little book on the subject.

MICHKA: The question you have not answered is how do you locate a good shaman?

VINCENT: Ah, that is super complicated. . . .

MICHKA: If you had some advice in this regard?

VINCENT: You have to see people who have already gone there. I believe that's the best way. People who have already been and are not trying to proselytize, in other words who are not trying to praise someone's merits, who are not under the spell of a shaman—and in whose personal everyday lives a discernable benefit can be seen. I think this is the best guide. Make sure the person is not completely out there, or thinks he is the reincarnation of Captain Haddock.* When you are able to see at the end of six months, a year, two years that the person has gone through an intense experience and came back intact, that's a pretty good clue.

---

*[A character from the *Adventures of Tintin*—a popular comic strip series in France and Belgium. —*Trans.*]

TWO

The Mysteries Encountered

JAN: It seems to me after rereading this book that we already have something here that is pretty unique in the sense that it offers a lot of little tips for anyone who might be curious or even tempted to try the experience. It is not just a kind of Backpacker's Guide to Ayahuasca, but a bit more: "Here, keep your eyes out for this, watch out for that; things are okay there."

How to begin a session, how to experience it, how to pay attention to your thoughts afterward. All these things are clearly present, and you never find this kind of stuff in books; that's what makes this an interesting document to me.

THE VISIONS

JAN: While rereading the book, I thought of some other things. Ayahuasca has a therapeutic, medical side too. But because it is a plant of power it has its negative side, and the fact that we point this out in the book and discuss it is really good. But for someone who is only going to go there not for a profound initiation but simply to get rebalanced and healed, this can help create a situation. . . . There is the risk that you are going to be confronted by dark visions at a certain time during the experience. Because our culture doesn't educate us about this, we are not going to see these dark things as our property but stick them outside right away. I've seen this a lot with people who have taken ayahuasca.

They say: "I saw horrible things; it wasn't coming from me; it was trying to get in." Whereas they are psychological thresholds, in fact. The shaman introduces dark things to you so you can purge and vomit them out, to cleanse them, to share them with the spirits, and you mustn't dive right in and squirm in pleasure; you have to let them travel through you. So, don't think that they are outside, but what you're seeing is a part of yourself. I ask myself: If my mind was in contact with my small intestine or liver, in touch with the awareness of this intestine or liver, what kind of head would it have? It would probably be like the sea monster heads some people see. They're not negative, just very primitive. . . .

JEREMY: Or even snakes.

JAN: You're right. Or even snakes. I think it has been said before that there is no reason to be scared of them. . . . So, if you even see spiders or dark things, you might be in contact with a part of yourself that is ill, you could have an archetypal connection with an organic part, a very primitive organ or one from which muted and simple desires are aroused. This is when you have to just relax and allow the thing to go through you, not think: "That's enough, I am being attacked by the shaman who is bewitching me instead of healing me." The reason is that this will make us send extremely negative energy through our thought to the person treating us, and in the final analysis that will be of no help to anyone. So when things like this happen the best attitude is to continue maintaining your well-being, don't ever try to push the darkness outside. Simply decide that the darkness we see belongs to us. This is how we won't sever ourselves from the shaman's healing by sending him a rejection of his action.

VINCENT: What you say is absolutely correct. During an ayahuasca session you are reasoning with different parts of your being, your consciousness, which are going to materialize in different kinds of visions. These visions can be totally terrifying or absolutely unthreatening. This is not a big deal; it forms part of the therapy or the system that ensures you make progress because it gives you access to dimensions of yourself, or consciousness in general, which you really have to face. While the experience may be strong or hard for a while, it's a natural part of any kind of shamanic work and you shouldn't be scared of it.

JAN: I have actually heard people say during a session: "Today, dark things were all around me; something was done to me." In fact, they have only been brought to where they feel pain—it forms part of the healing process. If you haven't been prepared, you will have a hard time accepting that it is you. People have no trouble accepting light, but they have a hard time with darkness.

JEREMY: I think when a person takes a substance like ayahuasca, his defenses go down and his psyche is almost naked, and the individual becomes vulnerable at this moment. This means that if the person administering the ayahuasca—who may not necessarily be a shaman— starts playing power games, a person who has not been prepared and unable to protect himself can actually receive a negative impact at this time.

It is a good idea to play things down and simply let people know that this is an experience that exposes an individual; you are stripped almost bare and placed in the hands of the person managing the session. There are cases of people who have been left unsettled following dubious treatments, and it is a good thing to know.

JAN: Hence the value of paying attention to the person you choose when you look to try traditional indigenous medicine. Approach people you trust and who have a certain . . .

JEREMY: Integrity?

JAN: Yes, integrity.

JEREMY: And purity of heart.
    [Silence.]

VINCENT: So, I suggested that we spend part of this time talking a little about the idea of God. I know that my feeling about God is not necessarily the same as it was before. The other theme I've proposed is that of creation.

JEREMY: Creation in the sense of the world or of a book? Creativity or the Whole?

VINCENT: A bit of both, in fact. Seeing how you are able to integrate into creation. I am interested in learning what kind of relationship you had with God before these experiences, if you had one. . . .

THE IDEA OF GOD

JEREMY: Yes.

VINCENT: What was it like during, what has it been like after? Did it change how you felt; did it change your conceptual system? Because I found Guillermo's response quite interesting.

JAN: What did he say?

VINCENT: During a lecture he gave in Paris, someone asked him: "Do you believe in God?" and he answered: "I believe in everything." That's really the answer I've come to today, and it seems quite real. . . .

You take it, Jeremy.

JEREMY: All right, fine. In fact, I have just been able to practice on this subject because I just got back from Croatia and the Croatians are very Catholic, and even if they are anthropologists and interested in molecular biology, once you touch upon life's mysteries, you have to talk about God. The truth for me personally is that I have become agnostic. This wasn't the case during the period of my first ayahuasca experiences, and I feel okay about sharing it; but first I want to explain my present point of view, not the one I had twenty-two years ago.

I think that when you talk about any concept, for example, "intelligence" or "consciousness," or words like that, it involves paying close attention to their origin and all the cultural baggage that goes with them. God with a capital G is the monotheist concept, often presented as a masculine force outside of the plant, a sort of unique entity who would be Intelligence with a capital I, who would be behind the Whole, and in whom you had to believe.

My one-thousand-four-hundred-cubic-centimeter brain finds this a weird concept. It seems obvious to me that all kinds of intelligences exist in the universe, in the plants, in anything you like. But I ask myself, in a sort of epistemological modesty: Is this something I have any chance of understanding? If you think about the human brain, you will see just how complex the neuronal patterns are, and you will tell yourself that the human brain hasn't a chance of understanding itself. What's more, we are very, very far from doing so. If forced to bet, I would bet that the human brain wouldn't manage to comprehend itself—but fine, it's already an act of faith to make this wager.

There are so many mysteries and things now that still remain to be understood; I ask myself: What purpose does making these acts of faith serve? Let's accept that there are many things we don't understand, and, if we want, let's try to understand what we can understand. So, personally, I am more interested in knowing than in believing, and especially not believing in things that I have trouble conceptualizing.

So, getting back to God with a capital G, the Great One in the cosmos—maybe he exists exactly like this and I am just a little too crude to get a good handle on it. . . . But yes, this is a concept I question. And when you see the animist peoples who do not have this monotheist concept, who are much more into plurality, they live within biodiversity, and there is a multiplicity of spirits and immaterial intelligences in their cosmologies. In fact it is much more diffuse rather than concentrated into one single entity.

So, already for the question: "Do I believe in THE monolithic God with a capital G that Judeo-Christianity has concocted for us?" Well, I prefer to reply that I know I don't know, that I am agnostic, and allow myself to challenge this kind of concept. While recognizing the right of each individual to believe—whether it is in the most militant atheism or the most committed Christianity. Furthermore, I find all sorts of good things in faith, a true faith—Christian, let's say, or Muslim—practiced with fervor. This can certainly lead to a respect for life. We've also seen that this can be abused every which way.

So, when you talk to me of God, it's "Here is this difficult mono-lithic concept." Besides, everyone gets all worked up when you start talking about God.

VINCENT: And what have your experiences with ayahuasca changed for you?

JEREMY: It's true, thank you: we can get to the bottom of this. . . .

I grew up in a Catholic town in Switzerland, although I came from an Anglo-Saxon Protestant area of Canada. My father was an atheist and my mother an Anglican, and by growing up in Fribourg, I actually went to a Catholic school and could see Catholicism right up close. I would have liked to believe in God, in fact. It is clear it held an attraction. . . . But in the end, I became a Marxist. I think that Marxism itself is a kind of faith, the desire to improve the world.

And it was through arriving like a kind of post-Christian, Marxist anthropologist among the Ashaninca practicing shamanism that I made contact with their very concrete manner of approaching what we call the sacred, in other words, well, the plants and animals are our cousins, and we have conversations with them in altered states of consciousness. And it is true that the ayahuasca experience I describe in the first chapter of *The Cosmic Serpent* convinced me in a highly visual fashion that there was another level of reality that escaped our rationalist, materialist gaze, and I could no longer deny it, because I had seen it.

On returning from two years in the Amazon and on returning to this rural, Catholic Switzerland from which I had come, I actually had bursts of enthusiasm to go to the monasteries, to visit the people who knew the sacred here in Europe to see . . . to see to what extent it was shamanic or not.

It so happens that I was living in a farm several miles from a Cistercian monastery and I spent a day or two with the monks. But it didn't really work out. I did not really find the shamanic side and real contact by speaking with the monks. And it is clear that when you are dealing with priests of the Catholic Church, often they are people who are going to tell you: "Because the Pope says that yoga is not good, well then, yoga is not good." And why is that? "Because it turns you within whereas God, specifically, is on the outside. . . ." We are a thousand leagues here from a spiritual sensitivity to the environment.

In fact, I have almost built myself a way I can understand the world by combining shamanism with rationalism. That's to say they are reading grids—not belief systems. Of course, you can argue that believing molecules exist is a belief. In this case, yes, I believe molecules exist; and therefore I believe in rationalism as a system of knowledge. And in the final analysis, yes, it is a belief system, too. But it is a verifiable one.

And when you put together what shamanism reveals about other species and about ourselves, and you reinforce it with the reading grid provided by science, I find that we already have more than enough mysteries to try and understand. Mystery is 99 percent of what's around us. Contemplating this mystery with joy is a form of joyful, agnostic spirituality.

VINCENT: And you, Jan? [Laughs.]

JAN: With respect to ayahuasca, what has it changed about my perception of God, right?

VINCENT: I don't know. . . . What would you say about God?

JAN: First of all, one of the first things that ayahuasca did concerning these big subjects was that it allowed me to see that being a nonbeliever was a manipulation of a thought system.

You have people who say: "I'm not a believer." But believing in the deductions that you can make based on the experiments of concrete science and on suppositions concerning the ultimate reality is to believe in these suppositions. So, it is a manipulation of the system of materialist thought to separate believers from nonbelievers: there are only believers.

I had to wait for ayahuasca to discover this simple thing, and I think it can be discovered simply through contemplation.

So, right off, this made me move on to the idea that, on this planet, we were all believers and were unified by this; and this was joyous. Next, with regard to God, I would say it is not so much as a concept—because the notion of concept comes from our society and our way of grasping the world, of our religions, and so on—I would instead say "feeling." And I would go toward the heart. That is to say that today I understand when someone talks to me of God. Before I did not understand, and I found it was something people talked about a lot and was something a little too big to talk about.

But I can understand when I hear people in New Orleans who enter a trance or who perform Gospel, and say: "I am in the feeling of God, and in the feeling of love, in the heart, so, I am there with God." I really like the idea of combining God with love and the heart.

When you are truly bathed in a feeling of love, you feel connected to everything else. I really loved this kind of thing, which I encountered before in traditional India and grasped by following Amma. Some people say she is a kind of avatar of God. It doesn't necessarily give me lots of confidence when someone is introduced to me as being an incarnation of the divine on Earth. On the other hand, by spending time with her and seeing that she was fully immersed in her incomparable flow of love for me, I saw her as a human being at a place that I am capable of attaining at times but not as much as she is, so she is closer to this feeling and closer to God than I am.

And finally, to return to the notion of concept, inasmuch as we still talk of concepts, I really like the Hindu concept of Shiva Shakti. This means that God is the dance of moving creation. God is everywhere. It is simply perceiving at a specific moment the beauty of a sign, the world, things, a relationship to a plant, to a natural phenomenon, to a being, to a piece of music, to a creation, to a movement. In other words, the whole of creation. There is no separation between creator and creature, that's all. I really love this idea; it brings you back to feeling.

I believe that this is the maximum point of my exploration of God,

from an intellectual point of view because—I alluded to this earlier—
one of the things that shamanism has done for me is that I had many
metaphysical questions when I turned to it. "Why does something exist
rather than nothing?" "Does God have choice?" "Who are we, who am
I?" "What is infinity?" The list can go on and on! We are all aroused
by our intelligence to raise questions that are beyond the ability of our
intelligence to answer. And specifically, in ayahuasca, to try to boil the
feelings you've had down into terms of concepts, because we are used to
having a relationship to the world along these lines.

After an eight-year practice with ayahuasca, I have noted that in the
major experiences—I am going to be a bit provocative here—not the
ones where you meet God, but, let's say, the ones where you encounter
feelings and where, to the contrary, you receive information, well here,
you are no longer asking these kinds of questions. In fact, I ended up
examining the matter extensively and never had any questions about
God from the mental perspective. On the other hand, I have told myself
the experience will go better by being more in a feeling of love. As for
creation, since that is the second half of your question, one of the things
that is a form of visual poetry and that I've always had a hard time
encapsulating in words, in thoughts, is this idea that, for me, returns
cyclically in the ceremonies—this idea that everything is connected.
There is a kind of immense joy in . . .

We are the creators of a universe in movement; you are the artisan
of this. In your very depths, in the depths of your DNA you possess
the intelligence that causes it to reproduce in two cells, which creates
this body and this intelligence. So you are holding all the secrets of life
inside. And what it tells me is about responsibility, both positive and
negative, which makes me very sad. In other words, I have the sense
that we are responsible both for everything good on this planet and
for everything bad, collectively, culturally, historically. We're carrying
everything.

So, we have to cleanse ourselves of the sorrow caused by negative
things. These are things that can painfully swallow us when looking
at the world. This is what the invisible looks like; and I would say in

conclusion that all of this is simply a way to get you to pay attention to your thoughts.

It's very sensible, in fact: your thoughts take action, and your actions take action. This progression is always there: action comes from thought. You think before you act, so, pay attention to what you're thinking. Then trace it back; the thought occurs during a moment you are feeling something and has a relationship to memory and to the other, to the world. So it is first going to come from a feeling. So, the closer you mesh with the rightness of a feeling, which is that of the heart or love, the more of this you let flow into your emotions, the more your thoughts will be correct. So, pay attention to what you do, what you think, in anger, in pain, and everything.

Of course, I still have a lot of work to do in this regard! But that's how I see it.

VINCENT: Well, I do not have much to add, right now. . . .

JAN: You were curious, in fact! [Laughs.]

VINCENT: No, but I think you said all that quite well. I concur with both of you. And I think God exists. He is quite real insofar as there are an enormous number of people who believe in God on this planet; this necessarily creates an extremely strong conceptual being. Talk about God to anyone on Earth and this will evoke something.

But there are other realities in which I happened to realize that the concept of God had no meaning because you are actually either employing a more refined perception or are one with something that makes it so God has no more meaning.

So, to sum up, I, who was very much a believer before all these experiences, am now much less of one. Or let's say that my faith has become . . . perhaps more relative. It depends upon the systems in which I find myself. And I adhere completely to what you said about the strength of the heart, which is something to which we can collectively connect.

JEREMY: It is true this is a vast subject. For example, you spoke of the intelligence in the human body: you follow a cell that comes from an egg and next . . . It is a mystery how an organism, which is the product of so much intelligence, can be so stupid sometimes. [Laughs.]

How is this possible, given all the intelligence in life, that we can be as stupid as we are? Here is a mystery that dogs us permanently. The other thing can be examined historically: the same culture that came up with the concept of a monotheistic God has also deluded itself spectacularly a number of times. For example, by saying that the Earth was the center of the cosmos. Or that man was above all other creatures.

Now, it is true that we know more with the discovery, in 1953, of DNA, in other words an enormous text written in a chemical language, which is in fact bordering on nanotechnology. That is to say any narrower, any smaller, and it would not work. If you are a molecule capable of storing information and capable of acting through autoduplication, you must be ten atoms wide. If you were eight atoms wide, this would not work, you would be unable to separate the strands and bring about reproduction, it would be too close to the immaterial.

If you wish to remain in the material world, you could not make anything more sophisticated in the field of miniaturization. And we know that this coding system and chemical alphabet is four billion years old. This was discovered in 1953. Hold on! We hadn't thought of this. Let's pretend that this took place on another planet and that we were just talking about a troop of apes; so there were apes who scratched their heads in 1953 and then discovered this enormous text inside themselves. And so was it their God with a capital G who had written this four billion years earlier? Is this proof of God's existence?

Then the atheist materialists said: "No, to the contrary, DNA proves that we are right, insofar as information is material, dear friends. We have discovered the genetic informational molecule. It is a molecule. We have won!" And the monotheists for their part were rather silent. They did not say: "It is God who wrote DNA." Salvador Dali said it in his inimitable fashion: "DNA is the proof of God's existence." [Laughs.]

And in fact during the 1960s, we discovered that it was not only an informational molecule, there is a genetic code that goes with it, and this genetic code is analogous to the codes used by human beings, which is to say that the individual letters have no meaning. The A, G, C, T molecules have to be combined in units of three for a meaning to emerge, and this corresponds to twenty amino acids and two punctuation marks: Start, stop. This resembles a code, dear friends; and it is a code. Until the discovery of the genetic code in the 1960s, the presence of this kind of code was considered to be proof of intelligence because, it was thought, only human beings used codes whose individual elements were devoid of meaning. This was a Saussurian code.

So let's examine the data: inside of us and inside all forms of life there is a coding system and a large text. We can scratch our heads and ask ourselves who is behind this. Clearly there is an intelligence. Telling yourself that all of this is the result of chance is something you can do, but it is a belief. The data indicates that what we are dealing with is a text and therefore an intelligence behind the text. So, to bring this flourish to a close . . .

When you consider just how much we were fooled and to just what extent we are only now discovering these things and that we have not even yet truly begun posing questions because all of this is somewhat taboo, we can tell ourselves: "We are not the center of the universe. Perhaps there are other coding systems in this universe; perhaps, yes, there was a great intelligence that created DNA but perhaps there is another great intelligence, or several others, who have written other systems, and perhaps we are not done yet, we have not reached the end of surprises in this cosmos. . . ." Then perhaps this God with a capital G exists, perhaps there is yet another entity behind DNA, perhaps there are still all kinds of things. We are just on the verge of understanding, so certitude is not appropriate.

VINCENT: It's just common sense, obviously. . . . I don't remember if I said it in my book, but these experiences have thrown me back into my own stupidity, permanently. Because it confronts you with something that does not exceed understanding so much as strengthens its complexity.

JEREMY: Someone once said that agnosticism was the sole honest intellectual position, that is to say, you admit that you do not know when it comes to ultimate causes.

JAN: Concerning what you said, because here you are going back . . . there is something I discovered only a year ago, here again, it is something that is ultrasubjective.

A year ago, *grosso modo,* people would talk to me about different things, which I could believe or not, or find interesting, but there was one thing from which I kept a certain distance—on the credibility of the thing as information—and that changed during one of my journeys and at the end of a ceremony: it concerns myth.

For me, there was the reality of the birth of the universe, the physical reality, the big bang, Planck time, those kinds of mysteries, and then, on the other side, there was a lot of stories people told each other, but were just one of the ways man was able to poetically compose his fantasies about creation. I was thinking of the myths of the indigenous peoples because they are completely fantastic stories. Today I think that myth is true. I think that myth is an exploration as important as science for the origin of the world and universal causalities; I believe that it is a kind of poetic language as in these very sensitive domains, the only person able to get near is the poet. Furthermore, the scientist going back to Planck's time says that equations turn into poetic trances. So, there you have it. Telling myself that myth is true, psychologically, as a Westerner, was too hard a path to take for years. I always listened to these stories with a small reservation in the back of my mind about their limits, while today, I have a much more direct relationship because of those ceremonies whose visions gave me the impression I was dealing with a mythological slide show.

You take years to reach the idea that the territory of dreams is a territory of experiences from which you can bring back information about reality, so you are no longer capable of telling yourself: "It is just a dream." The world of myth has become the order of a certain reality for me—of course it is not the material reality—but a certain reality of my psychology.

JEREMY: Claude Lévi-Strauss spoke about that fifteen years ago when he said that scientific data had achieved complexity of hallucinatory proportions. . . . If we simply speak of the quantity of information contained in one DNA molecule of a human cell, we have to visualize one thousand five hundred encyclopedia volumes in two-millionths of a pinhead. You can put this into numbers, but if you put images on top of it, it becomes mythological. And it is only the mythological, the hallucinatory, the fantastic that exceeds all understanding that is up to the task of doing justice to the data provided by science. So Lévi-Strauss states that science should put itself into the form of myths in order to be more comprehensible. Until that time, people had said: "Myth is what is false and science is what is true." Henceforth science needs the mythological.

[Silence.]

JAN: That's that. God, it's done! [Laughs.]

JEREMY: Next!

[Silence.]

JEREMY: It is a privilege having things transcribed, but having read the first part I have become more aware of the fact that what you say is one thing and how it appears on the page is another. . . .

VINCENT: That's for sure.

JEREMY: And with that fresh in mind, although I just shared my deepest thoughts about God and agnosticism, I would like to make it clear that I think those involved in religion are often very good people. And as you said, the enthusiasm around Gospel . . .

And it's not only because Gospel singers are cool. It's not because I declare myself agnostic and find this the most constructive way to proceed that there are not other roads to Rome. The important thing is specifically the ecumenism; and I find there is nothing more joyful, as an agnostic, than to have a dialogue and a friendship with someone who sees things differently. So, long live difference! Long live tolerance and ecumenism!

And there are so many mysteries that the fact there are a multiplicity of theological points of view seems a necessary thing to me, one to be encouraged.

JAN: Since you're saying that . . . [Laughs.]

It is true that I realized over time that there are no rules. I am still going to offer a counterexample: there are people who have adopted a belief system, so they are going to take certain actions for certain objectives. I would simply say it was for their karma. In any event, this is not as beautiful in the final analysis as someone who does not believe in God, in nothing after life, in nothing after death, and is still going to invest his time and energy helping the human, the planet, and the other. And that in this case, his thought is pure because it is placed in matter, in this world here, and comes straight from the heart; it is simple and not specifically spiritualist, religious, or what have you. So what I ultimately found out was that there are people who are atheists and more spiritual than some people. . . . You know, more with the spirits as they conceive it in the Amazon model. To be with the spirits, in other words the heart, simple thoughts of joy, of life, of others.

JEREMY: Atheism is an act of faith. . . .

JAN: Yes, precisely.

JEREMY: . . . A relatively courageous one.

JAN: Here, I think we are politically correct and consensual. [Laughs.]

JEREMY: Okay!

JAN: So then, that's taken care of.

JEREMY: Creation, creativity.

VINCENT: It also seems to me that we have spoken about this with regard to the difficulty of integrating the experience mentally. Being able to express things creatively in this reality has actually been a really great foundation for me.

JEREMY: I have a question for you because I read *Iboga* with a great deal of admiration, and I particularly liked the style you used to talk about iboga and initiation. I found it playful and mischievous. . . . So, did the shamanic experience alter the way you write, or did you always write so well?

VINCENT: Err . . . I cannot answer you on my qualities of style, which are relative all the same, but, conversely on the fact that I am mischievous and playful. So, if you like, I think that if I had not had this inside me, the book would not have had this coloration because what I experienced during my initiation was not at all of that nature. You can truly be full of admiration because the way . . .

JAN: He suffered like hell but turned it into a fun thing! [Laughs.]

VINCENT: Yes, and all the reservation you might have about iboga initiation comes specifically from that.

JEREMY: Let's say that my question was not gratuitous but means to say: Is this the writing style of someone who has gone outside and above himself and provided a bird's-eye view of our entire ridiculous side, and then reintegrated his body with his writing style . . . so does the playful side come from the experience of displacement due to shamanism . . . or not at all?

VINCENT: No, not at all. I have always had this sense of displacement.

JEREMY: So this is something you fell into when you were little?

VINCENT: Listen, I think I've always taken things like a joke. It is the opposite in fact. My experience with iboga does rather tend to make me lose, if you like . . .

JEREMY: Your sense of humor?

VINCENT: My sense of humor, yes! [Laughs.]

JEREMY: You don't want to be a killjoy. . . .

VINCENT: For a simple reason like you said: I think that when you have this kind of experience, you are going to resonate with your surroundings. For example, if you take ayahuasca here, it is not at all like taking it in the Amazon. I strongly believe in the fact that you are going to resonate, at a certain moment, in a given time-space, with what is there. It is very much like the way you describe it: every human body is the bearer of memory.

DIFFERENCES
BETWEEN AYAHUASCA AND IBOGA

VINCENT: I think that one of the differences between iboga and ayahuasca is that with iboga you are really going to touch this in depth; in other words, iboga is truly going to peel you apart almost cell by cell and is going to read your memory. Doing it in Africa really confronts you with the birth of humanity. More than South America, in my opinion. In any case, this is how I felt it. And because of this, you are going to stumble upon things that are terrifying because of their archaic nature: moments when you enter your primal impulses, moments when the life impulses and the death impulses completely overlap. There is a kind of savagery that is no longer even savagery but—how to put this?—a natural barbarism. That's to say you think you're seeing the life impulse, and you don't know, it doesn't even know what it should do. Should it live, should it be light or darkness, does it have to eat the other, should it fuck this other . . . ? It is really a kind of magma, in this particular instance, a kind of primeval magma.

My ayahuasca experiences have been fairly simple. They were kind of hard; I saw snakes, okay, super; I figured out the tricks, the configurations. With iboga, it was really a lot more profound, it was like I was really being shown the beginning of life. There is nothing, then there is everything. . . . And what do you do with it? You are woven from all of this. This isn't a kind of phantasmagorical world where you see visions, but right here, today, with both feet firmly planted on the ground. And it makes you tell yourself: "These are your brothers, and they are black;

look at how they live, they are still in the jungle, and you are exactly the same, or anyway this is where you come from." And it is where we all come from. It is necessary for you to confront this: how you constructed yourself, little by little, what you have done with this life that has been given to you, finally all this questioning; and you really are starting from the beginning. You're confronted by the human being, with all that entails. And I should say that the sense of humor does not necessarily exist when you are in that dimension, it has not been invented yet, so you actually have to juggle when you're there. . . . [Laughs.]

So, to answer your question, no, it is not necessarily thanks to iboga that my writing was so lively in the story of my initiation. But, getting back specifically to these round trips, what I find so extraordinary in the experiences that can be had today is that we are capable of making real leaps in space and time that were impossible before, unless you were Marco Polo. . . . You see how people lived ten centuries, twenty centuries ago, and two days later you are in Paris. You can use all this to arrange your own little personal deal to keep growing a little more, and I find this truly extraordinary. It's an experience; its level of spiritual understanding and knowledge, it is exoteric or esoteric, doesn't matter. Today anyone can have this experience and benefit from it, in my opinion. Keeping in mind the precautions we discussed earlier. I say this so I can finish on a positive note and prove I'm not just a killjoy.

JAN: To add a small commentary on what you are saying, not about the part on African humor but about the Amazonian part. I have always found a large dimension of humor in ayahuasca, even during the most terrible moments. On the other hand, since we've said a lot of different things in this book that will ultimately give people conflicting information on this subject, I want to mention a trick that I noticed, which I don't think we mentioned earlier: for example, you are talking about ayahuasca, you then say that ayahuasca took you somewhere, but it is primarily iboga that really introduced you to the mystery; and you'll see people that tell you the exact opposite.

VINCENT: Of course.

JAN: And whether things you tell me about iboga are the same things I find in ayahuasca. So, it is only alchemy. In other words: how you behave, how you accept the treatment of this healer or that plant in this or that country. The big mystery is how your personal alchemy, your history, is going to react to this. It's easy to try ayahuasca and have no visions, nothing happens. Then you have a great encounter with another plant or with a tradition that does not include plants. This just means that a person's personal alchemy is also going to be an essential factor. Generally speaking, you're going to know really quickly if it is possible for you to communicate with this plant and this culture, or if you need another plant, another culture, another way of looking at the world.

MORE ADVICE

VINCENT: Have we talked about what it means to have experiences in different traditions?

JAN: No.

VINCENT: Because this, too, is very important. What you say is right on. We're concentrating on the plants but I am very interested in other traditions, and traditions have brought me quite a lot.

JAN: We did talk a little about this: Zen for you, Vipassana, at one time. . . .

VINCENT: I think that people can raise questions. For example: If they are in X initiatory tradition and wish to go take plants, is that a good idea? For some this can be a very good thing, because, for example, initiatory plants are going to awaken you, sharpen your perceptual countersystems or your energy bodies. And then you have other people for whom this will not necessarily be a very good thing because, to the contrary, it can destabilize them. You have initiatory systems that completely object to plants, and others that can integrate them. So, here again, I don't believe there are any rules, mutual agreement seems to be the rule of thumb here, and you should not hesitate to ask the people initiating you your questions. I don't know what your thoughts are on this?

JEREMY: I think this is something fairly complex: what kind of advice to give people you don't know; it is problematic. If I consider my own experience with hallucinogenic substances, since we are talking about the subject, I have never read a book that offered advice. We did them completely unauthorized, among friends; we were unaware and took risks, we did things that I would not advise anybody to do. But by making mistakes, we learned, we initiated ourselves.

It is clear that by going to the Amazon, we realize, on seeing how the indigenous people proceed, that we others, hippies of the Western suburbs, had a lot of things to learn. In the meantime no one gave us any advice. I chose to follow my own path, and here I am.

I think that everyone follows his or her path. The advice of a little manual for hippies published by an alternative press during the '70s, for those taking LSD trips, was: "If the little voice in the head tells you, when everyone is going to take LSD, 'Ah, today, I don't know if I want to,' well listen to the little voice." When in doubt, abstain, in other words.

So, personally, give advice to people I do not know . . . No!

VINCENT: I don't agree with you, and I'm speaking from experience. I think you have a technical expertise, based on the traditions—but I could be wrong, again this is a subjective thing.

I think every tradition has a way of coding the energy of your energy bodies in accordance with the stage you have attained; once you know how to manage your energy a certain way, you can really get into a thing. You can be at one stage of a specific work in a tradition in which, for example, the fact of taking ayahuasca or another initiatory plant is going to alter this; which is not necessarily true in an absolute sense. Once you have gotten past a certain stage it is generally more of a nuisance, and I am not talking about people who are a little like dilettantes but . . . There are a fair number of people, for example, who do yoga a lot and have asked me: "If I take ayahuasca or iboga, will it not . . . ?"

I haven't been able to answer them. If they are truly working with a master teaching them a tradition by making them perform a certain kind of exercise, a certain kind of breathing every day while saying: "There, I am opening your energetic center, there, you are going to reach this energy level," and they take ayahuasca, it might be a good thing or a bad thing. Everything depends, I think, on the energetic centers you have developed. And that is a purely technical detail. . . . Anyway, that's what it seems like to me, hey, I could be wrong.

JEREMY: Who is up to making a diagnosis like this?

VINCENT: The master who is teaching you, normally—because you can also have a clique thing going on. When you are following a teaching you will get people telling you: "Hey, ayahuasca is the best thing; hey, yoga is the best thing. . . ."

JAN: And six months later, that's changed!

VINCENT: Six months later it has changed, but it seems to me that this doesn't bother some people at all, quite the contrary. It might be an enhancement they are able to juggle, while it might completely overwhelm others. People I've met have discussed this point. So, to conclude, there is no good or bad, it just depends on the individual. As Jan said, it depends on your personal alchemy, and if you have someone teaching you, you must see a priori if the teachings are compatible.

JAN: I have just one thing to show, precisely, that we are not going to avoid giving advice by giving advice. You mentioned that advice for trips from the 1970s: "If you hear the little voice, listen to it." That was the advice then. Fine, it's your choice. But if you're taking a traditional medicine path, when you hear that voice, ignore it, that's my advice! [Laughs.]

Because it happens all the time! In other words, on the evening you planned to have this experience that is intended to heal you, restore your balance, and let you embrace the indigenous world, the night you are going into the maloca, especially if you haven't eaten, you are going to be bombarded by the outpouring of thoughts: "This might not be a very good night to do this. I should really wait till tomorrow." And you will have these thoughts every night. I still have them! In this particular instance, you should just snuff them out, that's my opinion. [Laughs.]

I have a story about a person who came with me to the Amazon. When we got to Lima, this guy began feeling nervous. He was a little scared but at the same time he was completely drawn to the experience. To cut it short, we got down there. First night, he did not want to come and stayed in bed. On the second night I convinced him to come listen to the songs at least—we were only going to be there for a few days. On the third day, I said to him: "Come on, you have to at least try." And he went into such a state of fear that at eight o'clock he was in his bed with lights out, saying: "No, I won't budge!" [Laughs.]

This individual was fifty years old though, so I said to myself: "Fine." I was a little . . . disappointed. I said: "Frankly, you should at least try one mouthful, it is almost symbolic."

And then, that evening, I went through a very strong and very hard experience. And I saw things about fear, I saw the fear that held him prisoner; I met it in a different place and in a different way. And because of this, the next day, I had a lot of compassion for this person, and I told myself: "He is completely in the grip of something that doesn't want to let him go, something I've met."

JEREMY: You spoke to him about it?

JAN: I told him, yes, that I had been scared and that I had seen the fear that held him. And I think that one day . . . He wants to return there. He is drawn to this as much as he is repulsed by it.

JEREMY: Did he explain his fear?

JAN: He was scared of seeing things inside him. He had experienced extremely strong traumas. The fear you have, when all is said and done, is of yourself. You're scared of being scared, and I think, to the contrary of that 1970s manual, you have to act as a warrior to deal with this fear, you have to trust and get into the experience.

Now, if the next day you're a little upset, or the session ends on a kind of sour note and you're still scared, and haven't felt good during the day, you should ask yourself if maybe instead you should let things settle down and only take it again two days later when you feel better. But you should know for sure during the morning. You should remember the state you were in when leaving the session: this is the state that should serve as your guide when deciding whether to go back or not. It's not the state you're in five minutes before taking it, because fear is always connected to that state. Always.

VINCENT: To conclude, what I want to say is . . . It's really subjective; it's what I felt or what I thought I understood. Starting from the moment you think you possess a kind of truth, that's the time when you're actually no longer in the truth.

JAN: Absolutely. This is a thought that must be heeded. You may not be well because you have reached certain conclusions: you are in the grip of a certain force, power, that is going to make you sick because you are not right with the experience. You are going to be sick because the way you think and act is sick. This is not a witchcraft problem; it's a matter of how you put yourself back together after the experience.

VINCENT: In any case, it amounts to the same thing. Let's accept that witchcraft really exists; you can be bewitched. . . . Okay, the spell can be taken off you, too, you know. People can also manage their negative energy. Witchcraft is never a case of someone projecting something good upon you. Later, you can take this thing and turn it into something positive. . . . It forms a part, as you said, of the warrior way. And being able to specifically reflect back something luminous instead of evil is what healers do. A healer takes the sickness, sometimes he takes it inside himself and transforms it simply by recycling an unhealthy energy, or maybe an energy that doesn't fit into a certain context.

JAN: Well, for me, my gimmick, the Oncle Paul* gimmick, the little piece of advice, hold on . . . [laughs], is that I never think about it.

This means to say that when I feel a negative thing, I never let the idea of witchcraft take root in my mind because that would make it stronger. So, I tell myself that all my problems come from me. I try to resolve them within. And when things happen—in the Amazon you witness certain things, as you said—well, in any case, I work to keep them from forming any attachment to my thought, to my mind. During, after, during the remainder of the experience and your life. It's how you can protect yourself: if you don't give this kind of thing any faith, it cannot afflict you.

And the fact is that it's us, Western civilization, who are the teachers of witchcraft. When someone says: "That guy, he's a manipulator, he gets people all muddled, he takes advantage of them . . . ," when you say something like this, you are casting a sacred spell because this changes the way people are going to behave toward that person, and what he will have to live through.

We are all witness to a gigantic shamanic combat that is continuously going on in our world because we are not taught to pay any attention—again—to how we project negative energy through malicious gossip. An annoyed mother telling her daughter: "Stop singing, you are singing too shrilly," although she is only eight years old, is casting a spell on her; she is putting a demon inside her who is going to prevent her daughter from singing the rest of her life. People don't pay any attention to what they are saying or what they are doing, so we are the masters of that.

VINCENT: This is why I am coming back to this business of creation, which has been quite important for me: the act of writing, the act of making films. . . . It allows you to rewrite all this energy, whether good or bad, in a joyful and positive manner.

---

*[*L'Oncle Paul* was a long-running French comic strip about the learned and wise Uncle Paul, who would seize on the foolish and inane comments of his nephews as a pretext for providing didactic lessons on history and so forth. —*Trans.*]

JEREMY: I recently read a review of your latest film *99 Francs,* a film I really enjoyed; it is playful, mind-blowing, all sorts of good things. It was a review not even a paragraph long in a leftist French newspaper. . . .

JAN: In *Libé?*

JEREMY: And the first sentence: "This film is a piece of shit that blah-blah-blah" . . .

JAN: ". . . made by poor druggies," yes.

JEREMY: So, obviously everyone is free to not like a film. But that you can simply be seated there and say that the work of others, "bah," even if lots of other people are going to like it . . .

"Me, I declare that the creation of someone else is worth zero," is witchcraft, I agree with you. And I find it intellectually shocking. [Laughs.]

JAN: That is one of the choices a society makes. For example, you have a space in a newspaper; you can decide: "I am going to defend the movies I like, and I won't even talk about the ones I don't like." And since you have referred to this article, well, it demonstrates the witchcraft of our world. At the same time, it is freedom of the press, it's called democracy, it's the ability to say everything and that's important. Afterward, the individual has a choice to make, what kind of energy you are going to put into your words.

[Silence.]

I wanted to say something to put in as a preamble: "Although you have read this book, you won't understand the experience unless you try it." We talk about it, we have adopted an attitude that ensures that while a person may not know this experience through his own experience, this book can serve as a guide by providing intentions and sensations; however, it cannot give him a very clear idea or close approximation of the experience because it is so vastly different from everything we know.

JEREMY: Here, we are talking about swimming; but going swimming is something else entirely.

JAN: Exactly. It is amusing because I had the idea of an example that was: let's imagine that we are a society that lives only in the desert. There are guys who do books about the sea—okay, we're doing a book about the sea. But nothing equals going to see the ocean and immersing yourself in its waves; this will teach you a whole lot more. . . . I say this not to offer any kind of incentive, of course! [Laughs.]

JEREMY: A manual for Bedouins on how to bathe in the sea. [Laughs.]

EXPECTATIONS AND MISCONCEPTIONS

JAN: We always have received notions about what constitutes the reality of an experience. For example: I am going to look for a traditional shaman so I can have a traditional experience, because it is an ancestral thing after all. . . . I'm already expecting some kind of cliché image: the jungle, you speak with sign language, you wear traditional garb, you arrive at night and the rain is beating down on your tent, there is no electricity, and so forth. Because there's always a cliché that goes with anything. You are going down there; you have to have something like this.

This thought occurred to me because I saw the reactions when I was at the Spirit of the Anaconda Center this summer, which is a place in the jungle near Iquitos, where Guillermo has established a traditional medicine center. I saw the people when they got there say: "But I was told about a village and I have come to a place that looks almost like Club Med, it's not at all traditional, there are spick-and-span bungalows, a cafeteria, toilets, and now even a swimming pool. . . ."

VINCENT: Oh really?

JAN: Yes. And so you have the impression of being in a tourist trap. You say to yourself: "This stinks. This isn't traditional." And I want to say you have to dump all your preexisting images. Say you arrive at this center, for example. I shouldn't exaggerate, it's not Club Med; but it's close when compared to going to a real jungle community to take ayahuasca or a polluted city like Pucallpa, or some hard to reach village where communication is difficult and where there are a lot of social problems that are going to take up the bulk of your time psychologically before you even get to the experience and that will ensure that you come to the maloca worn out. . . .

In this particular center you're going to have a super traditional thing (we knew Guillermo in the city of Pucallpa, behind his house, and all). You are going to come to a place where you will be much better protected because you are in nature but in a much more comfortable environment. The same Indians are there, and from the moment you enter the maloca, the light still goes out wherever you are. You may be in the depths of the Amazon region, it's still the same place. And the rest of the time, physically, psychologically, you can recharge your batteries and concentrate on the experience, yourself, and your relation to nature, all at the same time.

There are people who make a U-turn and leave again saying: "This is not traditional." While I find it to be the ideal setup for traditional medicine to work best for a Westerner. Instead of arriving at the maloca exhausted and almost sick, dragging your feet, in the communities of San Rafael or Nueva Betania or along the Ucayali.

You can go into the villages of course. It is also quite beautiful: taking a boat, entering the communities, meeting their shamans and doing ceremonies with them. It is important for meeting a culture; it's a different relationship. Someone who discovers a bond with ayahuasca will have to expand his knowledge of the culture at some time; and it is not in Iquitos, for example, that he will find this culture. He must go to another city or into the villages. But for those people who are coming just to discover ayahuasca or just get a first taste of the region, they don't need to hunt for the traditional-traditional side lost in the depths of the jungle, because they think this is where it has to take place. You have to forget all your preconceived notions and go into these places you've heard about without any preconceived notion, including any about shamans.

There has been much talk about the shaman: we often project the idea of the wise Indian and are then surprised, because people behave differently. We confuse medicine and wisdom, even if there is wisdom in this indigenous medicine. But they are still different things. I would say that you shouldn't project a preconceived idea in this area and think you will have a much more traditional ceremony if you are in the depths of the jungle, where one might actually stumble upon a shaman who is much more a novice, for example. That's just how it is, there are no rules.

JEREMY: There is something to be said about how people can be mistaken by presuming to know what "traditional" truly is. Quite frequently there is the case of Westerners who set foot there and state that the people with whom they are dealing are not "real Indians." This forms part of the Western imaginal realm, but this way of looking at things is also fairly violent. It disqualifies an entire range of people and reality is often much more complex. Just one ethnographical example: the Cocama in the Peruvian Amazon.

They are a people who, it seems, changed their language in the sixteenth century after their first contact with the Portuguese on Brazil's Atlantic Coast. They abandoned their own language to adopt the indigenous lingua franca of another tribe so they could engage in trade. Then, in the eighteenth century, they emigrated two thousand five hundred miles into the Peruvian Amazon.

They were therefore already speaking a foreign language, but people said that it was their mother tongue, and they made this change a second time, during the twentieth century, by dropping their language for Spanish while saying: "We are not Indians, we are mestizos like everyone else. We don't speak an Indian language; we speak Spanish."

And during the 1980s, when the law said all at once that the people who were indigenous had rights to a territory, the Cocama said: "All things considered, we are the Cocama Indians." And now they are in the process of relearning their mother tongue, which was already, in fact, an adopted language. And what is traditional for this particular people since they made contact with Europeans is to be in transformation and to adopt the language of others and engage in trade. And, in fact, they are completely indigenous, and completely hybrid and modern within that process. That's the way it is. Who are these white green-horns who come down and say: "These people are not true Indians"? That is a seriously colonial attitude.

JAN: You mean to say that their tradition is the power to change, to go from one to the other, to customize their tradition?

JEREMY: Yes, exactly.

JAN: That's interesting.

JEREMY: Furthermore, they are far from being alone in this ability to transform. And if you look closely, during the traditional era, the sha-mans and indigenous peoples tried to transform into jaguars, the most powerful entity not under their control in the world around them. Now they are trying to transform themselves into gringos; gringos have replaced jaguars as the most powerful entities not under their control in the world. It is completely analogous. And this indigenous desire to be less traditional and more like the gringos fits into this tradition of a world in transformation.

JAN: This point of view never occurred to me.

JEREMY: And what complicates things is that after five hundred years of a relatively unprecedented colonial violence, where the people were even run over . . . Okay, I am not going to remake history. Finally, the ayahuasca tourists, of which I am one, show up and say: "We're ready, for the first time, to pay you for indigenous knowledge." And rather than look down on them and attempt to be missionaries and to change them, we are ready to put ourselves on the same ontological footing and receive a teaching. "Instruct us, if you please. Here is fifty dollars."

And if we look at these last five hundred years, we see that being ready to enhance the value of indigenous knowledge is rather a fine thing. While one may deplore it being done in a spirit of individual commercialism, these are the game rules currently in effect on planet Earth. So, it is okay that we can pay for indigenous knowledge and give it a market value, and that ayahuasca sessions have become a product. And I think it's important to be aware of this connection, even if it has the air of being a bit vulgar. Some may complain: "Yes, the true shaman is above money; once you give money, you contaminate the indigenous reality. Ayahuasca tourism is something we should be ashamed of."

There are people who contact me—more and more, by the way—and say to me: "I would like to go try ayahuasca, but I don't want anything to do with ayahuasca tourism. Could you advise me about a real shaman with whom I could work alone and not in a group with other gringos . . . ?"

In fact, the question is absurd; in other words, all of us together make up the mass of ayahuasca tourists. We cannot escape these circumstances and these realities, and it is a good idea to be aware of them. Furthermore, as consumers we also have a role to play: don't pay too much but also don't pay too little; be demanding about the level of certain standards. It is not only a deplorable reality, the commercialization of ayahuasca in the western Amazon.

JAN: They are going to make a Michelin Guide to shamans and places: three stars, four stars. . . . [Laughs.]

VINCENT: Yes, that is what we have begun doing with Caro. . . .*

JAN: I'm joking, but what you say is true. I, too, have gotten that: "I don't want to go there because there are too many people," and similarly: "Money is sleazy." And I tell you: that is a projection of Eastern spirituality. And that is not what this is about: it is medicine. And when you visit the doctor, you pay. If we remember that this is a traditional indigenous medicine, the relationship would be normal, like with a doctor.

It is ridiculous sometimes, the people arriving at the center who say: "Oh no, this is too touristic, I am going to go home." While I've known ayahuasca in the remotest villages . . . I am not going to paint a romantic picture, but there are things that are worthy in themselves as subjects for a film. It's wild, you arrive soaked to the skin by the rain to a little

---

*[Marc Caro is a French filmmaker and cartoonist. —*Trans.*]

maloca in the depths of a village that you had a hard time finding, and you went to all that trouble looking for their healer. But out of all these experiences I've gone through, I'm always happiest when going back to the center, because then I have a bit more comfort, my relationship with ayahuasca there is purely traditional, so it's solidly built, and someone is there who is familiar with Westerners, and I think this is a good thing, too.

It is true that sometimes there are around twenty people with you, most of them Westerners. So? When I was in Pucallpa there were twenty Indians and I was the only white person, or there were two or three. So? It is a collective thing. And it is good to see people of our culture come there. All this is a good thing.

VINCENT: Another thing, the quality of the shaman has no connection to this. In *Wizard of the Upper Amazon,* Manual Cordova-Rios tells it very well. When he left his tribe in the jungle, he arrived to find people who did not know how to prepare ayahuasca, who made it any old way. You can find villages where you'll see shamans of a very wretched quality.

JEREMY: Yes.

VINCENT: You can also find very good ones.

JAN: I have also received e-mails: "I want to do this really alone one on one." If you are sensitive to ayahuasca and there are forty people, you still have the impression of being alone with the shaman during the entire ceremony because there is the bond. You should not believe this is because of the setup; you must not confuse interior and exterior. That's just another way we project our concepts.

I personally realized this with regard to the indigenous people: sorrow at seeing Indians who were more Western than the whites and that you could sometimes get muddled up like that. I had too much trust in the indigenous people, in an unhealthy way for a while. Now I look at each person as an individual who has his way of thinking, created by a culture. But an indigenous person, when all is said and done, can be more gringo than a white in his way of looking at things, relating to things.

JEREMY: So, when the white person is playing Indian and the Indian playing the white person, who is muddling who up?

JAN: Yes, there is that, very good. . . . We are all Cocama in fact. With ayahuasca, I went through a period where I regretted not having dark skin. . . . I would have liked to be an Indian.

Good, after, the poor guy, when he is in the jungle and the weather is hot . . . You are not made for that from a genetic point of view. I come from the North rather, so I suffer. And afterward, it is a little like the questions about God: it all vanishes. You accept that you are a gringo, you will never be an indigenous person, you will never have an indigenous knowledge. But, on the other hand, you have super things in your culture, things you can take. Life is a journey, and you make it with the least number of projections possible.

JEREMY: And what do you both think, personally, of those Europeans who claim to be shamans?

VINCENT: I think everything is possible. You can have people with an inner gift, which reveals itself during an initiation; this doesn't have to be a paradox, in my opinion. It is all the same thing: I believe you have to see how they use it. To tell the truth, I have no set opinion on the matter.

You should be wary of people who delude themselves, of course. But I don't know; in the Amazon I have only known the rather "pure and hard" Shipibo.

JAN: Until fairly recently, I always had a tendency to say: it is quite simple; you are in a traditional medicine, it is a culture. To take the opposite case, it is like a surgeon who comes from the indigenous world and starts practicing surgery when he is forty. With empirical knowledge replacing years of medical study, you know what knowledge he's missing. . . .

VINCENT: Yes, that's so.

JAN: There are lots of levels in shamanism, but the white can't really attain certain truly advanced levels. Just like there are no indigenous people at certain levels in surgery, medicine, quantum physics. I have always told people to go see an indigenous shaman. A white person who cooks up his own recipe blending different spiritualities and religions, and the people who turn up there, put me on my guard. I just say be on your guard where this is concerned.

Now I am going to tone it down. I met for the first time—I asked him if I could cite him—François Demange, who is someone who has been working with Guillermo for ten years, and I did an entire series of very strong sessions with him and Guillermo. He came in at a certain time and sang for me, and it had a force. He sang in Shipibo, and I no longer knew if it was Ricardo or him who was singing me; I was obliged to open my eyes. It was the first time that a Westerner took me on a trip like that. So I told myself: "Hello, he is the first one I've met. He has the knowledge of an indigenous curandero, and he is capable of doing a healer's work in traditional medicine." This was a discovery for me after eight years of lots of, hundreds of gringos who sang in the sessions, with whom you feel good things, good vibrations, but it is not at all the same thing as taking someone and guiding him with song through an experience in which there is clearly an uninterrupted strong interaction with the healer. So, this was a happy discovery for me as because of it, you have a Westerner who appears to know traditional medicine much more deeply than you; so, you can touch on certain things that you could not touch on with an indigenous person. You are going to learn things from the perspective of words. It is extremely interesting, this particular relationship with a Frenchman.

VINCENT: There is Eduardo Luna also, who has been giving ayahuasca for a long time; I took it once with him. Fine, he plays records for you, but it also works.

JEREMY: He actively claims that he is not a shaman. In fact, he states clearly that he is an anthropologist.

VINCENT: Yes, but he leads sessions.

JEREMY: Yes, but . . .

VINCENT: You mean to say that the term "shaman," if we take it etymologically, is someone who is capable of manipulating the entities of nature, things like that. Actually, I don't think that this would be very possible for a Westerner, unless it were not for the fact of being truly immersed with others. What you say seems completely consistent to me.

[Pause.]

JAN: We've covered everything, then?

MICHKA: Would you have something powerful to say to finish up with? A conclusion?

JEREMY: A conclusion, dear friends . . .

VINCENT: No. Unless it would be something along the lines that despite all the reservations I've mentioned, to encourage people who are strong enough to try this kind of experience. The reason is that it will open you up enormously. It pushes you out of an overly egocentric vision— finally, centered on a very reductive view that is that of the civilized human being today.

JEREMY: Let's say that this may be one subject that least deserves a conclusion as I think we are at a beginning, at the beginning of comprehending that the human race is planetary, and that there is a unity within diversity and we can unite our different kinds of knowledge. Westerners—like us—can go to Africa, or to the Amazon, and learn to see things in another way. We can grasp that it is possible to dialogue with plants, through plants. We are opening our concepts. We can dialogue with shamans in the forests and they can learn from us, and starting from the moment we leave our categories behind, the blockages that shaped us, well, we can transcend all that.

For example, we are only beginning to put together science and shamanism; who knows where this will lead. . . . So I find that this is rather a joyful thing full of potential. Obviously, there is not only good news, there is also complexity; but yes, it is important not to conclude.

JAN: On reading the book, I had the impression of one thing, concerning these phenomena that are conspicuously absent from our culture. It is this that fascinated me, and it was the reason why I found the film *Other Worlds,* which I made and which testified to it, interesting: it is not Jeremy's conclusions about DNA, for example, or Stanislav Grof, or all the highly skilled scientists whose paths I've crossed, or artists, or us, capable of discussing this for seven hours straight—it is not so much the nature of what one is going to say but seeing that these tiny creatures who have encountered this phenomenon within the indigenous peoples have devoted part of their life to it, their vital energy, and been able to find echoes of it in their culture. And it shows, it demonstrates, that this is something that has deeply marked our lives. . . . So, this is the concrete, truly concrete thing I have drawn from reading this book. So it is not to conclude, but to understand. You have to go there. . . . But it is inspiring. And history is on the march; that's what I hope.

[Applause.]

JEREMY: Vale.

JAN: Vale.*

VINCENT: Ah, yes to that.

JAN: Now it is time to read this over again. We have to try and keep it as live as possible. You know, there are words you have a yen to remove, and then you say: "Ultimately, it gives it a living aspect." So, try to touch it up parsimoniously.

---

*[Spanish for "good job" (literally "worth it"). —*Trans.*]

JEREMY: I took out quite a few of my lines I have to say, because as much as what you said appeared impeccable to me, what I said pained me equally. . . .

JAN: You see, that's a mistake, because I wanted to do that to my stuff, whereas I found everything you said quite interesting.

VINCENT: It was the same for me.

JAN: You are a lot harder on yourself than you are on others; it is only logical.

JEREMY: Fine, that's all the better then!

JAN: You see, I had onomatopoeias and other things I wanted to take out, and then Michka said: "No, no!" and I said okay. It is true that reading it really gives you the feeling of three guys having a discussion. There are two or three moments that made me laugh. It made me laugh because it is alive. It is a document.

JEREMY: At one time you talked about a novel you had written, you said: "This altered my way of writing for a while. I wrote a novel, mainly, which was fairly long, in which I tried to retranscribe this possibility."

VINCENT: Yes. . . .

JEREMY: And what did you call it?

VINCENT: *L'Effacement progressif des consignes de sécurité* [The Gradual Erasure of Security Instructions].

JAN: That is a super title! I remember it, I read it, it was good. There were even some people at the end of the novel who went to the premiere of *Other Worlds*.

VINCENT: That's possible. Yes.

JAN: Because he wrote it after Peru, and when I began this documentary I said: "In this novel the characters will attend a preview of the film."

VINCENT: You see this particular book, as I do typically, is a way of giving shape to my experiences.

JAN: That's really wild! And the new one you wrote? I find that when you read Vincent you see all his mischievousness; and at times we see it again, you fall back into your mischievousness, into your nature. But you are way more serious when you express yourself verbally than when someone reads you.

JEREMY: I find that he is the Hergé* of hallucinogens, with a Little Prince side, to boot. It is very strong.

JAN: There is a Hergé side, yes, and a Tintin side. Tintin in the land of mushrooms. [Laughs.]

VINCENT: Fine, it's true that I might be a little bit too serious concerning all these kinds of things but . . .

JEREMY: There he goes again!

JAN: Listen, I read the text; I found that actually, in the beginning, you tackle an incredible number of things, and then two to three times you just let yourself go talking about the benefit you got from them, and the reader gets a good feel for what it's all about.

VINCENT: There is a difference, if you like, between speaking for yourself—what you have gotten out of something for yourself—and then advising others about it. Being capable of guiding your thoughts and all that. If the experience worked . . . The world would still be a little bit different, eh!

MICHKA: What do you mean, "if the experience worked"?

VINCENT: If these experiences were fruitful and crowned with success. There is a group logic, as well. If all the people undergoing the experi-

---

*[Hergé is the pen name of Georges Remi (1907–1983), the artist who created the Tintin comic strip. —*Trans.*]

ence were credible, including in that dimension, I think things would take a different course. This experience would be credible and it would obviously be followed by others, which would be beneficial, and so on. There would be a snowball effect. Today, we could not say that this snowball effect would be in favor of this experience. . . . It is not completely convincing, right?

MICHKA: I am not sure I understand what you are saying.

VINCENT: How to put it . . . You see, I am always starting from this 1970s mythology where you had, hup, off you go, a total awakening of the human being, and it seems to me that this philosophy of opening, of progression, of higher consciousness, of awakening, is not, in bulk, super convincing at the moment.

MICHKA: You mean to say that you do not think there has been any increased awakening, overall, among the people who have had this experience?

VINCENT: These techniques are truly techniques of awakening; in fact, they show you other facets of the world. If they were well incorporated, incorporated in a positive way, they would have more success. Today they are not successful; there is a kind of interest, an infatuation, but this is not success. In any case in France they haven't had any success.

One reason is the fact they are banned. So you even have a government that has created legislation about a thing that could have been beneficial. This is not normal: if it is beneficial there is no call for a group to enact legislation about something and prohibit it. Something's not right there. Either it is beneficial or not. If it is beneficial, why prohibit it?

TIGRANE: At the same time, history shows that prohibition is not necessarily rational and that all sorts of likely beneficial things have still been banned.

VINCENT: Agreed, but in this particular case, the people who have gotten something out of it should make it a point of honor to . . . Look at Galileo, he still invented a system even if, at the time, he was censored and bullied. He was not burned at the stake, but in the end, it was close.

JEREMY: He retracted himself while saying: "And yet, it moves!"

VINCENT: It does not prevent the fact that the future proved him right. And I think that today, it must be made a point of honor to be as rigorous as possible because, even if it is not working today, maybe it will work tomorrow. This is the reason I take every precaution, to avoid speaking at cross purposes, if you like, when I say attention must be paid to dangerous sectlike activities.* One is the reason that it is true that there can be dangerous sectlike activities in these kinds of things; and two, it is the prevailing discourse.

I met people on the commission to ban iboga, and this was their first objection: "Ah, but there are the dangerous sectlike activities." Yes, there are cult dangers, but this is no reason to label something as bad. At the same time I try to preserve the quality of the experience, to not handicap the future, and then navigate the situation as it is. This is the reason I take so many precautions. No one can say today anymore: "It's brilliant, it works super well," because this is not true. But perhaps it will work tomorrow; finally, we have to hope it will. There are perhaps other things that will work. We should not focus exclusively on this one either; there are many ways of seeing things differently.

But if you like, I am more sensitive to this because of my history with iboga; because I happened to write a book about it, so I felt invested with a mission. One with the purpose of saying: "I have had a super experience, why don't you try it?" And when I look at why you are not trying it, it is because, it is obviously not a super experience for you. So, there you have it, it is a bit like the snake biting its own tail.

JAN: You can say that again. . . .

---

*[In France, unlike the United States where religious freedom is the law of the land, official government bodies exist to investigate "*les derives sectaries.*" —*Trans.* (with a tip of the hat to Jeremy Narby for his enlightening explanation).]

VINCENT: But I think we have found a good compromise here. We are creating a book that is not a television show addressed to the public at large but is still going to address a targeted audience, in which we all explain some of our views. It could encourage people to try the experience.

JAN: And for an appendix you can list the flights. . . . [Laughs.]

VINCENT: No, but even if people don't try this experience, it will make them see that . . . Jeremy, for you it is a little different, but Jan and I, with our histories, we are still looked at as crackpots.

JEREMY: Oh, err, me too, eh! [Outburst of laughter from everyone.]

JAN: And I think there are people who are going to read this book and say: "They are three crackpots. . . ." Do you give a damn about this?

VINCENT: I don't give a damn at all. You see, I was photographed in VSD, with my long hair and African clothes. . . .

JAN: Oh good. You're a seeker, too. . . . [Laughs.]

JEREMY: "Crackpot number 1!"

VINCENT: . . . While telling myself, if you like, that this could get things moving. I don't much care what people think of me, but on the other hand, this is in terms of effectiveness. And that is the reason I stress the serious side of the thing. And the school side would seem like a good trail to me. . . .

JAN: It's like going under the scalpel. You are going to be operated on. When you go into the anesthesia room, if you can say: "Fine, listen, tomorrow instead . . . I don't feel it, it's the anesthetic. Tomorrow!" And off you go. It is the same thing. It's a medicine; it is serious business. It is an operation. . . .

VINCENT: Yes, that's for sure.

JAN: On the mind, the soul, but it is an operation. It is still a heavy thing; it's not four guys dropping acid in their pad. So, it is normal to be scared. Me, I don't like it when I go to the dentist and have to open my mouth. Finally, that said, I experience less ecstasy at my dentist's, whereas there, in that particular instance . . .

On the one hand, it is the drill on the soul, on the cavity of the soul [noise of a dentist's drill]; and then, on the other, it is the ecstasy, that for the time being, I've never experienced at the dentist's.

JEREMY: The cavity of the soul . . . Me, I'd rather go to that kind of dentist.

JAN: Ah, in the Amazon! [Laughs.] You have some cavities on your soul. . . .

JEREMY: I don't think so, but we'll see. . . . You never know, exactly.

JAN: There is a thing, hold on. . . . But maybe we've talked about it already; you manage to bring very little back from ayahuasca into your natural state. For example, you may feel you are a complete master of your feelings and emotions, and two days later enjoy a kind of peace, and then go off at the smallest detail of everyday life, not necessarily into a rage, but into things. . . .

This is very hard, because these are very remote states. On the other hand, when you are going through a drama, like a car accident or something quite intense, there, on the other hand, it will come back. When you are in great danger, your attitude, everything comes back. I was, at one time, attacked, not so long ago. . . .

VINCENT: Oh really?

JAN: Yes, a person walked up to me and said: "I am going to kill you," looking me straight in the eyes, from about a foot and a half away. Anyway, I had the impression that I froze like a snake, because, all at once I was . . . Don't send any negative signals.

VINCENT: Where was this . . . ?

JAN: In the metro. Fine, he was probably just bragging; he probably would not have killed me. But it was a tough experience. At once, I was completely clean as a pin: I got through the thing by giving off peaceful signals, having a calm voice. . . . Whereas I am capable, when I don't manage to find my keys, when I have to leave and I am running late, of getting real irritable: "Hey, where did I put my keys?" and things turn into a drama. You see, because these are just damned silly little things. The place where I most saw the work of ayahuasca was when my father died. I believe I spoke about this, no?

MICHKA: No, you didn't talk about it.

JAN: Well, this was really a big life lesson, because when you are with someone, your father . . . I don't know if you both have your two parents.

JEREMY: Yes.

JAN: Afterward, you tell yourself, there are two categories: those who have lost one of their parents and those who haven't—a little like those who have taken ayahuasca and those who haven't. It is one of the major experiences of the initiatory life. And so, when I spent ten days by his side while he was dying, well there . . . I was totally like in the maloca, but in life.

That is what I have learned from these experiences that take you to the very bottom of your feelings, that dig into your feelings so deeply that you form a relationship, the plant guides you, the shaman guides you, the healer guides you to have the right attitude. And there, I had everything that came my way, and these are moments in which you are filled first by a very powerful emotion and then by a very potent feeling, because you retouch all your memories.

You see, when you are fragile, when you are a child, your father, he is really a major figure. And so you are going to touch all that again, and your forgotten feelings will reawaken—those of the child for its father—because this is what you are in the process of separating from. So there is a profound sorrow that rises, even anger, and a direct, frontal relationship with death. And well, there, ayahuasca is . . .

Let's say, to make things simpler, that what I learned with the Shipibo allowed me to see the love that is behind this. In other words, behind the sorrow, you have love in fact; you see what inspired the sorrow, it was the immensity of the love between the being who leaves and the one who stays; and to stay in this feeling in order not to sink . . . This is truly worthy of an ayahuasca ceremony.

And one time I lay down in the bed next to him and I imagined my death, too, to share his awareness. These are things that come from ayahuasca, all that. All at once I told myself: "I want to be with him; therefore I also have to die." And I got into the bed next to him and remained by his side. These are really attitudes that come from my time spent with the Indians: how to get through life's difficult moments. And this helped me during those moments, the toughest moments.

Before, I thought, when someone who was seventy years old died . . . you know someone close loses his father or his mother at a certain age, it is a totally natural phenomenon. I saw the person who had collapsed or was deeply depressed for a year because of it, and found it hard to understand intellectually, telling myself: "It's a natural phenomenon, you have to get through it. . . ."

Once I went through it, I saw first of all that I had completely underestimated the thing's power, but at the same time I was able to deal with it during that time. You see, you allow yourself to go down instead of closing yourself off, you let yourself go down into your feelings, into your feelings, into your feelings. And ayahuasca gave me a lot of help, because mourning can be done in a beautiful way. On the other hand, I can still get annoyed because I've lost my keys!

People have asked me: "What did you bring back from these experiences?" And I would say, to be happier and have a better relationship with my feelings. That's it. That is a testimony to what it can bring to us. And I also found, really, having been in India, having somewhat studied the Tibetans, and peoples with another kind of relationship to death, that frankly speaking, we are not at all prepared for it in our society.

VINCENT: Yes, that's for sure.

JAN: Even me, who thought I was prepared, but was not. You are but not enough.

JEREMY: What is striking is that there is a denial of death in Western cultures, and at the same time, when you watch movies or television, there is a constantly growing pile of corpses. The dead are shown in fiction movies; the corpse is a kind of punctuation mark in the modern narrative, oddly enough.

JAN: Definitely. People even eat with a TV on in which . . . Boom, an attempt on someone's life. You see guys exploding in blood with an arm missing while you are stuffing your face. You, you're eating. So, there's something wrong with this picture. What's more, this is a question that's almost more interesting than the one about God, to ask ourselves, "What is our relationship with death?" Because we don't really know if some of us have met God while still alive, or will meet him after, but if there is anything we are sure of, if there is any one single thing that connects the whole of humanity together, it is death. Everyone is going to die. This is a real note of optimism because—

JEREMY: "Relax!" [Laughs.]

JAN: Put your mind at ease, everyone is going to die! So, all the more reason to drag ourselves to the Amazon to die a little, virtually.

JEREMY: Of course, exactly.

JAN: This will educate you because, frankly, we are not ready.

JEREMY: So, to work!

JAN: Learn to die. We are really out of it when it comes to our relationship to death.

VINCENT: Are you familiar with the books by Elisabeth Kübler-Ross? She did a whole body of work on this subject.

MICHKA: In any case, once someone is dead, quick someone takes him away, hides him, puts him in a box. We do not even see the dead.

JAN: Yes, I remember when I was little, I touched my grandfather. A corpse is . . . On the level of initiation we talk about going into the jungle, but when you find yourself confronting the moment of your father's death, and when you find yourself facing the corpse, looking at it . . . There you are receiving an initiation. Just like women receive an initiation by giving life. . . .

It is as if the world was made so you could be initiated. You still have to get through these kinds of moments and be guided in the initiation. And often after death we are distraught, at the death of another. And I understand. I tell myself that the tragedy I would not recover from is the death of one of my children. There, you are confronted by an unnatural death. I do not know if psychologically, despite everything I say I've learned, or think I've learned—there, I don't know if I am equipped to deal with that kind of thing.

With our position in the chain of life, we already have this possibility for initiation. But we are uneducated, or are not helped or prepared to seize this opportunity—if I can put it like that—this opportunity of initiation, in order to transcend. . . . That's the thing, we have to transcend. We don't have a choice.

This bothered me a little, but one of the things I wanted to do after my father's death was make a documentary on death. To go find healthy people and accompany them to their last breath.

And I got healing in Peru, also. I will not hide from you that when I went to Peru in July, I told myself: "Good, things are okay right now, I am doing well, but I am going to scrub a little because necessarily—you sense it—there must be something."

And it was incredibly good. . . . At one moment during a ceremony . . . I went within. I did not have an esoteric contact: I went into the feeling that connected me to my father, directly. And then the sorrow came. The sorrow . . . And when I almost let go . . . Bing, I went into love for the living, and there, Bing. I wove it around my companion, my children, and Guillermo. . . . And *bam,* and *bam,* and *bam* . . . And it was the same. I saw that it was the same but that it was active through others; that's what this showed me. As a result I emerged from the maloca having touched the feeling again and not having zapped the sorrow, but instead of diving inside it, I had seen it philosophically. . . .

JEREMY: So it could be integrated.

JAN: Yes, love is . . . it is the same in fact. It has a different color, but it is the same feeling. So go where there is a wound and go where there is good, in order to recharge your batteries. And I swear to you, it is very strange because at the beginning, what it wove together . . . The song wove the love already there, the bond I had with Guillermo. A trick of the heart, but coming from me, a thing of love, or recognition, super strong, moving. And I then said to myself: "Good, go on, it is working, buddy. I love you, I know you love me deeply; we are brothers and all but, fine, this is going to stop!" You see, there was this type of thing: "I am not going to collapse; I think about my father and I am not going to weep for the love of you just behind it!" This transferred to my companion. While there, it got even stronger, by the way. And then to my children, which was where the wave broke. . . .

And I think that here again, you know, people have prejudices. I thought I was going to have a more esoteric relationship, a more contact with the dead type of thing. But it was contact with feeling, the feeling of love.

JEREMY: "The vine of the dead" . . .

JAN: The vine of the dead, yes. And the living.
    [Silence.]

JEREMY: Bueno, amigos. Gracias. Thanks for the get-together.

Glossary

ayahuasca: Beverage made from different hallucinogenic plants, traditionally consumed by the shamans of the indigenous peoples of the Amazon. In these Amerindian communities, ayahuasca is used to go into a trance for divinatory purposes or as a healing tool.

ayahuasquero: Indigenous or mestizo healer who ritually consumes ayahuasca to acquire knowledge.

bwiti: Initiatory rite native to Gabon, centered around the manducation of iboga roots. The etymology of the word *bwiti* means "emancipation." *Bwiti* would therefore literally mean "that which permits man to gain his freedom."

curandero: Traditional healer of South America who treats both physical and spiritual illnesses.

DMT: Dimethyltryptamine is a hallucinogen naturally present in numerous organisms ranging from plants to human beings. It is one of the active ingredients of ayahuasca, but it can also be synthesized. In its pure form, it is crystalline in appearance and produces, when smoked, an almost immediate and extremely powerful hallucinogenic effect of short duration.

iboga: Root consumed in the context of traditional rites mainly in Gabon and Cameroon. At high doses, iboga causes strong feelings of nausea, vomiting, and a state of muscular asthenia in which numerous visions appear.

icaro: Icaros are the songs that shamans use as a communication technique with the other beings of nature. They also serve in a very precise way to influence the consciousness of a human being that has been altered with psychoactive plants.

maloca: A large hut in which the ritual ingestion of ayahuasca takes place.

peyotl: A small cactus without spines, considered as sacred, which brings on an altered state of consciousness and is ritually consumed by some Amerindian groups. They also employ peyotl (peyote) as a kind of universal remedy.

San Pedro cactus: Tall column-shaped cactus with few or no spines that is 10 to 20 feet high and found in the central Andes, in Ecuador, and north of Peru. It is a plant that alters consciousness and is utilized by some shamans.

sensory deprivation tank: A hermetically sealed booth that contains a saline solution warmed to body temperature. Once the individual has lain down in it, he or she floats there in darkness and with the absence of all sensation—practically no sense of touch. No light, no sound, and no smell. The result is an altered state of consciousness close to that produced by deep meditation.

shaman: An indigenous practitioner who has been alternately viewed by Westerners as someone possessed, a sorcerer, a medium, or a priest. There is in fact a good deal of versatility in his attributions, which are exercised in a ritual context inside his or her community. They can notably involve the ability to treat the ill or to cause harm to an enemy. To communicate with the spirits, the shaman enters a trance.

Shuar: A people of the Jivaro Indians who inhabit the jungles of the upper Amazon.

tobacco: The oldest and most widespread of all shamanic plants. Tobacco can be absorbed in the form of juice; its smoke is frequently blown on their patients by shamans.

toé: An Amazonian plant quite similar to datura, used for its hallucinogenic and medicinal qualities, and whose ingestion can be dangerous.

About the Authors

JAN KOUNEN, FILMMAKER

Jan Kounen was born on May 2, 1964, in Utrecht, The Netherlands. He studied at the Arts Decoratif of Nice (E.P.I.A.R.), concentrating on the domains of cinema, animation, and pixillation. He graduated in 1988 with a superior national diploma in plastic expression.

Filmography

Gisèle kerosene [Kerosene Gisele]. 1989. Short fiction film. Winner of the Grand Prize for Short Films at the Festival of Avoriaz.

L'Âge de plastic [The Plastic Age]. 1991. Short black-and-white fiction film.

Vibroboy. 1993. Short fiction film. Winner of the Prix de la Recherche at the Festival of Clermont-Ferrand.

Capitaine X. 1994. Short fiction film.

Le Dernier Chaperon rouge [The Last Red Riding Hood]. 1995. Short fiction film.

Dobermann. 1997. Feature-length fiction film.

Blueberry, l'expérience secrète. 2004. Feature-length fiction film. Released in the United States as *Renegades.*

Other Worlds. 2004. Feature-length documentary. Winner of the Grand Prize of the World Festival of Adventure Films of Manaus.

Darshan. 2005. Feature-length documentary. Official selection of the Cannes Film Festival 2005.

99 Francs. 2007. Feature-length fiction film.

"Panshin Beka winoni." 2008. Segment from the feature-length group film *Huit* [Eight].

Published Works

Visions: regards sur le chamanisme [Visions: A Look at Shamanism]. Paris: Editions Télémaque, 2005.

Darshan: voyage dans les bras d'Amma [Darshan: Journey in the Arms of Amma]. With B. Benant. Paris: Editions Télémaque, 2006.

99 Francs, le manuel d'utilisation de la société d'hyperconsommation [99 Francs, A User's Manual for the Society of Hyperconsumption]. With F. Beigbeder, S. Allix, and J. L. Planche. Paris: Editions Télémaque, 2007.

JEREMY NARBY, ANTHROPOLOGIST

Jeremy Narby was born October 23, 1959, in Montreal, Quebec, Canada. He has three children and lives in the Jura region of Switzerland. Holding a doctorate in anthropology from the University of Stanford, since 1989 he has been the director of Amazonian Projects for the NGO Nouvelle Planète.

Published Works

Indigenous Peoples: A Field Guide to Development. With John Beauclerk and Janet Townsend. Oxford: Oxfam, 1988.

Amazonie, l'espoir est indien [Amazonia: Hope Is Indian]. Paris: Favre, 1990.

La Vision des autres: les Amerindiens et la "découverte" des Amériques [The Vision of Others: Amerindians and the "Discovery" of the Americas]. Fribourg, Switzerland: Saved, 1992.

The Cosmic Serpent: DNA and the Origins of Knowledge. New York: Tarcher, 1998.

L'ADN devant le souverain: science, démocratie et genie génétique [Voting on DNA: Science, Democracy and Genetic Engineering]. With Jacques Dubochet and Bertrand Kiefer. Geneva: Georg, 1997.

Shamans Through Time: 500 Years on the Path to Knowledge. Co-edited with Francis Huxley. New York: Tarcher, 2002.

Intelligence in Nature: An Inquiry into Knowledge. New York: Tarcher, 2005.

Other Works

"Amazonia Ambient Project." Audio lecture. Presented with "The Young Gods" at the World Cultural Forum in Sao Paolo, the Jazz Festival of Montreux, London, Paris, Prague, Budapest, and Zurich, 2007.

VINCENT RAVALEC, FILMMAKER AND WRITER

Vincent Ravalec was born in 1962 in Paris. He has two children and lives in Clamart. An autodidact (he dropped out of school at the age of fourteen), he became an apprentice cabinetmaker, and he held various odd jobs until the beginning of the 1990s, when he began to write. He is also an assistant film director.

On publication of his first book, *Un pur moment de rock'n roll* [A Pure Moment of Rock 'n Roll], he enjoyed success, which only grew with the release of *Cantique de la Racaille* [Punk Canticle], which became a bestseller.

At the same time he began creating his own short films as well as several long films. He also writes songs (for Johnny Hallyday and Marc Lavoine). He has also written several screenplays and cinematographic adaptations, an activity he continues today in tandem with directing, as well as writes for the cinema, graphic novels, and literature.

In 2000 he began the literary series entitled *Le Jeu* [The Game], as well as a series of travel books. He is also working on concepts for a television series.

Filmography

Par-delà l'ère glaciaire [Beyond the Ice Age]. 1994. 3 mins., black-and-white.

Le Dur Métier de policier [The Difficult Job of Policemen]. 1995. 10 mins.

Joséphine et les Gitans [Josephine and the Gypsies]. 1996. 30 mins.

Cantique de la racaille [Punk Canticle or Canticle of the Riff-raff]. 1998. 90 mins.

L'Odysée merveilleuse de l'idiot Tobiggan (includes: *Les Mots de l'amour, Never Twice, Une prière vers le ciel, Portrait des homes qui se branlent, Le Masseur, Voyage sur la terre, Conséquences de la réalité des morts, Les Autruches, L'Amour dans les saunas, Pourrissures des putrefactions mortes, Attirances vers la vide*) [The Wonderful Odyssey of the Idiot Toboggan (includes Words of Love, Never Twice, A Prayer to Heaven, Portrait of Men Who Jerk Off, The Masseuse, Journey Over the Earth, Consequences of the Reality of the Dead, The Ostriches, Love in the Saunas, Putridness of Dead Putrefaction, The Lures of the Abyss]. 2000. 90 mins.

Les Arts magiques [The Magic Arts]. 2001. Ten 6-min. segments, documentary television series.

Une orange roulant sur le sol d'un parking [An Orange Rolling on the Ground
of a Parking Lot]. 2005. Directed by V. J. Milosh. 26 mins., experimental
film.

Published Works

L'Avenir [The Future]. With Patricia Reznikov. Bordeaux: Editions le Festin,
1997.

Les souris ont parfois du mal à gravir les montagnes [Mice Sometimes Have a
Hard Time Climbing Mountains]. With illustrations by C. Berbérian and
P. Dupuy. Paris: Editions du Seuil, 2000; Points Virgule, 2002.

Utilisation maximum de la douceur [Maximum Use of Tenderness]. With Lamia
Ziadé. Paris: Editions du Seuil, 2001.

Ngenza, céremonie de la connaisance [Ngenza, Ceremony of Knowledge].
Document. Photographs by Laurent Sazy. Paris: Presses de la Renaissance,
2004.

Le Doigt de Dieu dans un ciel tout blanc [God's Finger in a Completely White Sky]. Novels.

———. *Cantique de la Racaille* [Punk Canticle]. Paris: Flammarion, 1994; Paris:
J'ai Lu, 1999. Winner, Prix de Flore.

———. *Wendy.* Paris: Flammarion, 1996; Paris: J'ai Lu, 1999.

———. *Nostalgie de la magie noire* [Nostalgia for Black Magic]. Paris:
Flammarion, 1997; Paris: J'ai Lu, 1999.

Le Jeu [The Game]. Novels.

———. Adventure Book. *L'Effacement progressif des consignes de sécurité* [The
Gradual Erasure of Security Instructions]. Paris: Flammarion, 2001; Paris:
J'ai Lu, 2003.

———. Book of Rules. *Pour une nouvelle sorcellerie artistique* [For a New Artistic
Witchcraft]. Paris: Librio, 2001.

———. Magic Book. *Wendy 2 ou les secrets de Polichinelle* [Magic Book: Wendy2
or The Open Secrets]. Paris: Flammarion, 2004.

———. Book of Colors. *Une orange roulant sur le sol d'un parking* [Book of
Colors: An Orange Rolling on the Ground of a Parking Lot]. France: Au
Diable Vauvert, 2004.

———. Book of Divination. *La Vie miraculeuse du clochard André* [The
Miraculous Life of the Bum Andrew]. Paris: Flammarion, 2006.

———. Book of Initiation. *Bois Sacré.* With Mallendi and Agnes Paicheler. Vauvert, France: Au Diable Vauvert, 2004. Translated into English as *Iboga: The Visionary Root of African Shamanism.* Rochester, VT: Inner Traditions, 2007.

———. School Book. *PEP, Projet d'éducation prioritaire* [PEP, Plan for Priority Education]. Paris: Mille et une nuits, 1996; Ego Comme X [Ego as X], 2007.

———. Book of Healing. *Hépatite C* [Hepatitis C]. Paris: Flammarion, 2007.

———. Familial Book. *Quinze ans et demi* [Fifteen Years and a Half]. Paris: Flammarion, 2008.

———. Incredible Book. *L'Evangile du Verbe Pur* [The Gospel of the Pure Logos]. Forthcoming.

———. Literary Book. *Héros, Personnages et Magiciens* [Heroes, Personalities, and Magicians]. Paris: Fayard, 2008.

L'Accomplissement des prophéties [The Fulfillment of the Prophecies]. Novellas.

———. *Un pur moment de rock'n roll* [A Pure Moment of Rock 'n Roll]. Paris: Le Dilettante, 1992; Paris: J'ai Lu, 1999.

———. *Les Clefs de bonheur* [The Keys to Happiness]. Paris: Le Dilettante, 1993.

———. *Vol de sucettes* [Theft of the Lollipops]. Paris: Le Dilettante, 1995; Paris: J'ai Lu, 1999.

———. *Recel de bâtons* [Possession of Stolen Sticks]. Paris: Le Dilettante, 1995; Paris: J'ai Lu, 1999.

———. *L'Auteur* [The Author]. Paris: Le Dilettante, 1995; Points Virgule, 2002.

———. *La Vie moderne* [Modern Life]. Paris: Le Dilettante, 1996; Paris: J'ai Lu, 1999.

———. *Treize contes étranges* [Thirteen Strange Tales]. Paris: Le Dilettante, 1999; Paris: J'ai Lu, 2001.

Le Danger des courants électriques [The Danger of Electric Currents]. Digital TV editions. Photos by C. Mariaud.

———. *Portrait des homes qui se branlent* [Portraits of Men Who Jerk Off], 1995.

———. *Conséquence de la réalité des morts* [Consequences of the Reality of the Dead], 1997.

———. *Attirance vers la vide* [The Lures of the Abyss]. Forthcoming.

Nouvelles du monde entier [News from the Whole Wide World]. Paris: Editions du Seuil.

———. vol. 1. 2004.

———. vol. 2. Forthcoming.

Children's Books

Pourquoi les petit garcons ont-il toujours peur que leur maman les abandonne dans une forêt sombre et noire? [Why Are Little Boys Always Scared Their Mothers Are Going to Abandon Them in a Dark, Black Forest?]. With Anne-Marie Adda. Paris: Editions du Seuil, 2000.

Ma fille a quatorze ans [My Daughter Is Fourteen]. Paris: Librio, 2005.

Les Aventures d'Arthur et Violette [The Adventures of Arthur and Violet].

———. vol. 1. *Les filles sont bêtes, les garcons sont idiots* [Girls Are Stupid, Boys Are Idiots]. Paris: Editions du Panama, 2006.

———. vol. 2. *Le Président ne peut pas être un imbécile* [The President Cannot Be an Imbecile]. Paris: Editions du Panama, 2007.

———. vol. 3. *Bons à rien, prêts à tout!* [Good for Nothing, Ready for Anything!]. Paris: Editions du Panama, 2007.

Index

BOOKS OF RELATED INTEREST

Iboga
The Visionary Root of African Shamanism
by Vincent Ravalec, Mallendi, and Agnès Paicheler

DMT: The Spirit Molecule
A Doctor's Revolutionary Research into the Biology of
Near-Death and Mystical Experiences
by Rick Strassman, M.D.

Sacred Vine of Spirits: Ayahuasca
Edited by Ralph Metzner

The Psychedelic Journey of Marlene Dobkin de Rios
45 Years with Shamans, Ayahuasqueros, and Ethnobotanists
by Marlene Dobkin de Rios, Ph.D.

Plants of the Gods
Their Sacred, Healing, and Hallucinogenic Powers
by Richard Evans Schultes, Albert Hofmann, and Christian Rätsch

The Encyclopedia of Psychoactive Plants
Ethnopharmacology and Its Applications
by Christian Rätsch

The Shamanic Wisdom of the Huichol
Medicine Teachings for Modern Times
by Tom Soloway Pinkson, Ph.D.

Salvia Divinorum
Doorway to Thought-Free Awareness
by J. D. Arthur

INNER TRADITIONS • BEAR & COMPANY
P.O. Box 388
Rochester, VT 05767
1-800-246-8648
www.InnerTraditions.com

Or contact your local bookseller